UNIVERSITY OF NORTH CAROLINA
STUDIES IN THE ROMANCE LANGUAGES
AND LITERATURES

Six Historical Poems
of
Geffroi de Paris
Written in 1314-1318

Published in their Entirety for the first Time
From MS. fr. 146 of the Bibliothèque Nationale, Paris

and

Translated into English

by

Walter H. Storer, Ph.D., and Charles A. Rochedieu, Ph.D.

Of the Department of Romance Languages,
Vanderbilt University

CHAPEL HILL

NUMBER SIXTEEN   1950

TABLE OF CONTENTS

Introduction	v
Explanatory Note of the Transcription	xi
Les Avisemens pour le Roy Loys	1
De la Comète et de l'Eclipse de la Lune et du Soulail	42
Du Roy Phelippe qui ores règne	53
Note on the two Latin Poems of Geffroi	58
Un Songe	61
Des Alliés	73
La Desputoison de l'Eglise de Romme et de l'Eglise de France pour le Siège du Pape	81
Glossary of Proper Nouns	91

INTRODUCTION

In 1836 the famous French scholar Paulin Paris wrote: "Tels sont les ouvrages de Geoffrey ou Godefroy de Paris, qui *certainement mériteroient d'être publiés dans leur intégrité*.[1] The publication in full, as suggested by Paulin Paris more than a century ago, of the six historical poems in French written by Geoffroi or Geffroi de Paris is the primary purpose of the present work.

Paris had been describing the eight poems, six in French and two in Latin, found under the name of "Mestre Geffroi de Paris"[2] in the fourteenth century manuscript numbered "fr. 146"[3] in the Bibliothèque Nationale. The titles of these poems, listed in the order in which they appear in the MS., and with the approximate dates of their composition, are as follows:

1. Fol. 46-50. *Les Avisemens pour le Roy Loys.* 1314-15.
2. Fol. 50. *Du Roy Phelippe qui ores règne.* 1317.
3. Fol. 50, verso. *De Alliatis* (in Latin). End of 1316 or 1317.
4. Fol. 51. *De la Création du Pape Jehan* (In Latin). End of 1316 or 1317.
5. Fol. 52. *Un Songe.* End of 1316 or 1317.
6. Fol. 53. *Des Alliés.* End of 1316 or 1317.
7. Fol. 54. *De la Comète et de l'Eclipse de la Lune et du Soulail.* November, 1316.
8. Fol. 55. *La Desputoison de l'Eglise de Romme et de l'Eglise de France pour le Siège du Pape.* 1316-18.

The dates indicated are readily ascertained from the contents of the poems, as may be inferred from a summary (with interpolations) that Natalis de Wailly included in his *Mémoire sur Geffroi de Paris*[4]: "En résumé, la première pièce de vers [*Les Avisemens*] de Geffroi de Paris a été composée à la fin de l'an 1314 ou au commencement de l'année suivante [Verses 1259-63 of *Les Avisemens* indicate that the poem was written before the coronation of Louis X on August 3, 1315]; la seconde [*De la Comète*] est du mois de novembre 1316 [Verses 307-28 of *De la Comète* indicate that this poem was written after the birth of John I on November 16, 1316 and before the infant's death, several days later, was made known]; les autres sont postérieures, soit à l'élection [August 7, 1316] de Jean XXII [*De la Création du Pape Jehan*], soit à l'avénement [June 5, 1316] ou au sacre [January 6, 1317] de Philippe V [*De Alliatis, Des Alliés, Un Songe*, which three poems are addressed to King Philipe V], soit à la mort [February 18, 1317] du fils de ce prince [*Du Roy Phelippe*, which in verses 16-7 exhorts the king not to lament the loss of his son], et à cause des sujets qui s'y trouvent traités on peut croire que les plus récentes furent terminées en 1317 ou au plus tard en 1318."[5]

---

(1) P. Paris, *Les Manuscrits François de la Bibliothèque du Roi*, Paris, 1836, t. 1-er, p. 331.
(2) The author's name will be so spelled throughout this work, since it appears thus in the MS. It is given in the table of contents at the beginning of the MS., which contains other poems including the anonymous *Chronique Rimée* (or *Métrique*), now also ascribed to Geffroi.
(3) The MS. was numbered 6812 in the time of P. Paris.
(4) N. de Wailly, *Mémoires de l'Institut National de France. Académie des Inscriptions et Belles-Lettres*, Paris, 1849, t. 18e, pp. 495-535.
(5) *Ibid.*, p. 521.

Of the date of *Desputoison* de Wailly says that verses 258-9 of *De la Comète* inform us "que le Pape Jean XXII songeait à quitter la France. On peut donc croire que Geffroi de Paris composa vers le même temps la pièce intitulée: *Desputoison* ..."[6]

About the life of Geffroi, however, nothing is known. C. V. Langlois says that our poet "était en vérité un lettré, sans doute un clerc (voir les *Avisemens*). Voilà tout. De lui, on ne connaît, en outre, que ses opinions politiques, qui étaient nettement royalistes, cléricales, conservatrices; son caractère, qui était très indépendent."[7] But Geffroi makes no definite statement about himself other than to identify himself three times in the poems:

    1. Cil qui le fist si est ton homme.
       Geffroy de Paris l'en le nomme.
              Avisemens, ll. 1358-9.
    2. Natus ego G. de Parisio ...
             La Création du Pape Jehan, 1. 1.
    3. Il n'a mie .v. moys entiers
       Que je, G., tel songe songoie.
              Un Songe, 11. 46-7.

Geffroi's eight poems, although quoted in part a number of times, have never been published in full, up to the present time. J. A. Buchon, in 1827, seems to have been the first to publish excerpts from them. In the preface to his edition of the *Chronique Métrique* (or *Rimée*),[8] found also in MS. fr. 146, Buchon transcribes rather carelessly 138 verses from *Les Avisemens* and ten from *Du Roy Phelippe*. Paulin Paris, in the above mentioned description of the eight poems, quotes 131 verses.[9] Paris, however, did not read the poems very carefully, since he completely misinterprets the last verses of *Les Avisemens*, declaring that they prove that Geffroi was a "mesureur de sel." He praises especially the poem *Des Alliés*, a part of which (94 verses) he also published in the *Annuaire historique de la Société de l'histoire de France* for 1837.[10]

A decade later, May 28, 1847, de Wailly read his *Mémoire sur Geffroi de Paris* before the Académie des Inscriptions et Belles-Lettres, refuting Paris' statement that Geffroi was a "mesureur de sel" and undertaking to prove that Geffroi was the author of the *Chronique Métrique* (or *Rimée*). in Stating his argument, which is the accepted viewpoint of present day critics, de Wailly[11] quotes 124 verses of the six French poems and 13 verses from the two Latin poems.

---

(6) *Ibid.*, p. 520.
(7) C. V. Langlois, *Gefroi des Nés, ou de Paris, Traducteur et publiciste* in *Histoire Littéraire de la France, Ouvrage commencé par des Religieux Bénédictins de la congrégation de Saint-Maur et continué par des Membres de l'Institut*, Tome XXXV (suite du Quatorzième Siècle), Paris, 1921, p. 332.
(8) J. A. Buchon, *Chronique Métrique de Godefroy de Paris*, Paris, 1827, Pref., pp. I-VII. Buchon mentions only seven of the eight poems, since he fails to note that there are two in Latin. The *Chronique*, more fortunate than the authentic poems of Geffroi, has been edited two more times: It is in the *Recueil des hitoriens de la France*, T. XXII, pp. 87-166; and within the last year A. H. Diverres of Manchester, England, has completed a critical edition of it.
(9) P. Paris, *op. cit.*, pp. 325-36.
(10) *L'Annuaire historique de la Société de l'histoire de France pour l'année 1837*, Paris, pp. 156-71. This is included in a dissertation on the language of the trouvères. Paris here restates his idea that Geffroi was a "mesureur de sel."
(11) N. de Wailly, *op. cit.*, pp. 498-521.

INTRODUCTION   vii

The poems received very little attention from scholars during the second half of the nineteenth century. However, in 1901, in the Lavisse *Histoire de France* we find 31 verses, which Langlois[12] quotes together with many others from the *Chronique Rimée*. Twenty years later this same scholar gives the most complete summaries we have of the eight poems in the article,[13] already cited, wherein he seeks to show that Gefroi des Nés and Geffroi de Paris are the same person and the author not only of the eight poems listed under the name of Geffroi de Paris in MS. fr. 146, but likewise of "treize ou quatorze"[14] additional poems including the *Chronique Rimée*. In this article, 61 French verses and seven Latin verses from the eight poems and a considerable number of Geffroi's expressions are incorporated in the summaries of these poems.[15]

Finally, an American scholar, W. P. Shepard,[16] published in 1928 the entire poem, *La Desputoison de l'Eglise de Romme et de l'Eglise de France*.

This list of quotations, perhaps not entirely complete, indicates that only six or seven hundred verses (some of the listed quotations are of the same verses) of the 2687 verses of Geffroi's six historical poems in French have heretofore been published, leaving some 2000 verses to the obscurity of MS. fr. 146. That is a surprising fact, both from a literary and from an historical point of view.

It is true that some scholars of early French literature, notably Gaston Paris, have practically ignored Geffroi, but others, as Petit de Julleville, are more kindly disposed: "Geoffroi de Paris est, en réalité, le premier en date des nouvellistes parisiens, experts à résumer les faits du jour en petits vers prosaïques, mais coulants, vifs et malicieux, non sans charme. Son style, dont on a médit, est celui de fabliaux, et, si l'on veut, des mazarinades. Comment se fait-il que personne—non pas même ses éditeurs—ne se soit avisé de remarquer qu'il avait beaucoup d'esprit?"[17]

Although the critic had in mind especially the *Chronique Rimée* when he wrote the above lines, the style of the shorter poems in quite similar and would deserve similar remarks. But such is not the idea of Buchon, the first publisher of the *Chronique*, who says: "La première de ces pièces [*Les Avisemens*] est la seule qui mérite quelque attention."[18] Paulin Paris was a trifle more liberal in saying that "Sa profession [*mesureur de sel*, according to Paris' misinterpretation] ne l'empêchoit de faire d'assez bons vers."[19] Paris also characterized some of the verses of *Des Alliés* as "beaux."[20] De Wailly returns to the less favorable viewpoint when he says of *Un Songe* that it is "la seule [pièce] dont la lecture ne provoque pas l'ennui."[21]

It remained for Langlois to give Geffroi his due: "Comme ce 'Geffroi de Pa-

---

(12) E. Lavisse, *Histoire de France*, Paris, 1921, T. 3-e, II, par Ch.-V Langlois, pp. 122, 247, 272.
(13) C. V. Langlois, *op. cit.*, pp. 324-348.
(14) *Ibid.*, p. 346.
(15) *Ibid.*, pp. 327-332.
(16) W. P. Shepard, *Un débat inédit du quatorzième siècle* in *Mélanges de linguistique et de littérature offerts à Alfred Jeanroy par ses élèves et ses amis*, Paris, 1928, pp. 571-81.
(17) L. Petit de Julleville, *Histoire de la Langue et de la Littérature Francaise*, T. 2, *Moyen Age*, 2-e partie, p. 294.
(18) Buchon, *op. cit.*, p. VII.
(19) Paris, *op. cit.*, p. 328. (20) *Ibid.*, p. 334. (21) De Wailly, *op. cit.*, p. 506.

ris n'a pas encore eu dans *l'Histoire littéraire* la notice à laquelle il a droit, c'est ici le lieu d'examiner les problèmes qui se posent en ce qui le concerne, et son oeuvre."[22] Of the poem *Des Alliés* he says that "cette pièce . . . plus vivement et plus agréablement écrite que les autres, paraît être, jusqu'ici le chef-d'oeuvre de l'auteur."[23] Geffroi's style, he states, "est assez particulier; diffus, négligé, mais vif, avec abondance de proverbes, des locutions favorites qui reparaissent souvent, et, de temps en temps, à la rencontre, des formules bien frappées."[24] Elsewhere Langlois says: "la virulence de ces pièces n'est pas moindre que celle de la *Chronique*."[25] "Le style du chroniqueur présente d'ailleurs tous les caractères distinctifs qui s'observent dans les huit pièces. Toujours négligé, souvent plat et embarrassé, mais pourtant avec de la véhémence et de la vie; farci de proverbes: parfois comme haletant en raison de l'usage, voire de l'abus, des rejets. Çà et là, des images et des tours de phrases originaux qui, quoi qu'on ait dit, élèvent certainement l'écrivain au-dessus de la médiocrité."[26]

While there may be divergence of opinion on the literary value of Geffroi's poems, their historical value is certainly incontestable. After citing several passages[27] from *Un Songe*, Paulin Paris remarks: "On voit, d'après ces extraits, que la pièce ne manque pas d'importance historique."[28] In regard to verses 157-72 of *Des Alliés* Paris states: "Ces vers sont beaux et d'ailleurs fort importants. Comme leur date de 1314[29] est incontestable, ils prouvent qu'il faut au moins faire remonter au roi Philippe-le-Bel la réduction des fleurs de lis au nombre de trois. Ainsi on ne dira plus qu'un monument est certainement postérieur à Charles V, par la seule raison qu'on y trouve figurées les fleurs de lis réduites."[30]

N. de Wailly uses Geffroi's poems to prove the existence of the *ligueurs* or the *alliés* after 1314: "La durée que j'assigne au parti des alliés est prouvée, je crois, d'une manière évidente par les poésies authentiques de Geffroi de Paris. Et d'abord, il n'est pas douteux qu'il n'en fasse remonter l'origine au règne de Philippe le Bel. J'en trouve la preuve dans sa pièce du *Songe*."[31] After quoting verses 207-11 of that poem, he adds: "Voilà donc l'origine du parti des alliés clairement indiquée."[32] De Wailly's idea that verses 258-9 of the poem *De la Comète* inform us that the Pope John XXII was thinking of leaving France has already been cited.[33]

This same poem, because it apparently was written after the birth of the posthumous King John on November 16, 1316, and before his death several days later, suggests also the possibility that the news of the baby king's death was suppressed by the opponents of his uncle Philip V, who would not have been king if the child had lived. As it does not seem probable that Geffroi would have writ-

---

(22) C. C. Langlois, *op. cit.*, p. 327. (23) *Ibid.*, p. 330.
(24) *Ibid.*, p. 332. (25) *Ibid.*, p. 335. (26) *Ibid.*, p. 336.
(27) *Un Songe*, verses 1-3, 169-80, 210-3, 237-40, 299-303, 326-34, 337-51.
(28) P. Paris, *op. cit.*, p. 331.
(29) The date should be the end of 1316 or the beginning of 1317, since the poem is addressed to Philip V and not to Philip the Fair, as Paris thought, but the correct date is still long before the time of Charles V (1364-80, regent in 1356).
(30) *Ibid.*, p. 334. (31) N. de Wailly, *op. cit.*, pp. 505-6. (32) *Ibid.*, p. 506.
(33) *Ibid.*, p. 520, Cf. note 6.

ten his poem in three days, this apparent suppression of news might have been one link in the court intrigues against Philip, which led to the failure of many of the nobles to attend his coronation on January 6, 1317.

But even if no other authority had pointed out the historical value of these poems, the fact that they are used and quoted in the Lavisse *Histoire de France*, as is mentioned above, would be sufficient to prove their worth for historical purposes. In this standard history of France we find, together with the already indicated quotations of verses,[34] such statements as: "on connaît par des 'dits' et des chansons politiques de 1315 et des années suivantes les sentiments que les ligues de 1314 inspirèrent à la bourgeoisie parisienne, très attachée à l'idée monarchique. L'auteur du *Dit des Alliés* [Geffroi], entre autres, déclare que les 'Alliés' si fiers de leur 'noble sang,' ont bientôt révélé, par leurs actes, leurs intentions néfastes."[35] "Plus tard, l'auteur de la pièce intitulée *Un Songe* résumait ainsi le règne de Philippe IV: ce fut un temps où l'on chassa"[36] .... "L'auteur du poème intitulé *Avisemens pour le roy Loys*, dédié en 1315 à Louis le Hutin, exhorte ce prince à régner d'accord avec 'Sainte Eglise,' ce que le dernier roi n'avait pas fait; d'où les malheurs de son règne:"[37] ...

Since the historical value of Geffroi's poems is, therefore, quite manifest, a brief chronology of the royal and papal rulers of France during the time of the poems is helpful in order to understand them better: The three kings of the period were two brothers, Louis X and Philip V, sons of Philip IV (1285-1314), and John I, the posthumous son of Louis; and the pope was John XXII. Louis X (le Hutin) was king from November 29, 1314 to June 5, 1316, being crowned August 3, 1315; Philip V (le Long) technically became king on June 5, 1316, but acted as regent until the birth of his brother's child, John I, on November 16, 1316. After the three day "reign" of the infant king, whose untimely death occurred on November 19, 1316, Philip was again king until January 2, 1322, being crowned on January 6, 1317. John XXII was elected pope at Lyons on August 7, 1316, after an interregnum in the papacy of more than two years (Clement V, the preceeding pope, had died in 1314). John XXII, a Frenchman born at Cahors and one of the popes during the so-called Babylonian captivity (1309-1377), chose Avignon for his residence and was pope until 1334.

Largely because of their historical value it was deemed advisable to have this first complete publication of Geffroi's six[38] French poems accompanied by an English translation. This makes the poems more readily available to English speaking historians and may even suggest ideas about the meaning of obscure passages to French readers. The translation is not intended as an arbitrary interpretation of the poems and often other possible meanings are given in footnotes.

---

(34) Cf. note 12.
(35) Lavisee, *op. cit.*, p. 272. Verses 37-41, 43, 133-35, and 241-46 of *Des Alliés* are quoted on this page.
(36) *Ibid.*, p. 122. Verses 169-72, 179, 183-86, and 207 of *Un Songe* are here quoted.
(37) *Ibid.*, p. 247. This statement is followed by verses 458, 462-66 of *Les Avisemens*.
(38) The two Latin poems are not being published here.

The poems are being published in the order in which they appear in MS. fr. 146, except that *De la Comète*, which is next to the last in the manuscript, is placed after *Les Avisemens* to make the sequence more chronological. It is possible that *Desputoison* may have been written before *De la Comète*, since John XXII, the pope over whom France and Rome are disputing in the poem, was elected three months before the birth of King John I. However, because such a possibility[39] is highly improbable, the poem is placed last, as it is found in the manuscript.

---

(39) Cf. note 6.

EXPLANATORY NOTE OF THE TRANSCRIPTION

The poems are transcribed as precisely as possible from photostat copies of MS. fr. 146 of the Bibliothèque Nationale of Paris. Punctuation, apostrophes, division of words, hyphens, diareses, and such accents as are needed to clarify the meaning or to indicate the syllables for the meter, are added. In regard to the spelling of words, five rules are observed:

1. Changes in spelling are restricted to writing out abbreviations and contractions, and to distinguishing between *i* and *j*, and *u* and *v*.
2. All other words except those in brackets or those in parentheses and italics are spelled as in the MS.
3. Words which need to be corrected are italicized, and followed by the suggested italicized corrections in parentheses.
4. Several words, not italicized, are put in parentheses, because they are incorrect repetitions of the scribe and should be omitted in reading the poems.
5. Additional words, or letters, needed either for the meaning or for preserving the meter, are in brackets and are not italicized.

Capital letters except for initial words of verses, are only occasionally found in the MS. In the transcription, proper names of persons and places have been capitalized in accordance with modern usage, and in addition, *Roy, Royne, Emperiere, Pape, Eglise, and Sainte Eglise* are written with capitals because of the evident respect in which these rulers and the church are held by the author.

Through the observation of these rules the number of footnotes is greatly reduced.

In the English translation, words in parentheses indicate an alternate, generally a freer, translation of the preceding expression; words in brackets are added to clarify the meaning.

LES AVISEMENS POUR LE ROY LOYS

Mau vit, ce dit-on, qui n'amende,	Ill lives, so 'tis said, he who makes not amends,
Et en meffait ne gist qu'amende.	And in crime lies only atonement.
Pour ce, ne doivent pas les diz	Wherefore, "dits" (poems) should not
Estre diffamez, ne l'esdiz,	Be decried, nor the edict,
5 Où il y a à amender.	Wherein there is something to amend.
Quant l'en est prest de l'amender,	When one is ready with the amending,
L'en ne doit du tout contredire	People should not contradict in their entirety
Dités où il ha à redire;	"Dits" wherein there is something to criticize;
Ençois en doit-on le bien prendre,	Rather should the good be taken therefrom,
10 Et, ce qui fera à reprendre	And, what will cause reproof
Doucement mettre en verité,	Gently should be put in truth,
Et corriger en charité.	And corrected in charity.
Pour ce, le di qu'aucuns ditez	Wherefore, I say this: That some people
Aucuns ont fait, ou ont ditez	Have composed "dits," or have written
15 Moz, qui sunt en autre devise	Words, which are couched in other guise
Assis que raison ne devise.	Than reason dictates.
D'autres aussi, par couvenant,	Other [ideas] also, by common accord,
Si gracieus, si avenant,	So gracious, so charming,
Resont en ces ditez trouvez,	Are again found in these "dits,"
20 Qu'en les tient bons et esprouvez.	That they are regarded as good and tested.
Et se li Roys les vouloit faire,	And if the King were willing to carry them out,
En bien resnier n'auroit que faire.	To reason well he would have only to do so.
Et pour le Roys sunt-il escripz,	And for the King are they written,
Si doivent estre en ces escripz.	So, they should be in these writings.
25 En ces ditez, qui bien entendent,	In these "dits" those who understand well
Pevent veer qu'à .iii. fins tendent,	Can see that they [the poets] tend to three aims,
Ausquelles veullent exciter	To which they wish to arouse
Noustre Roy par leur reciter:	Our King by the reciting of them:
La premiere est de bien paier;	The first is to pay well,

ll. 1-6. The poet starts with the very "rich" rhymes of which he is so fond,—words of two or three syllables, alike in spelling, but usually differing in meaning.
l. 2, *qu'amende*. The *commande* of P. Paris is not justified by the MS.
l. 8, *Dités*. *Dit* and *dité* are used interchangeably for *moral poem*. It is not known to what critics or what "dits" our poet is alluding.
l. 10, *fera à reprendre*. *Faire* in a causative sense is used both with and without *à*. See ll. 53 and 54.
l. 19, *resont*. Cf. *refu*, *La Comète*, l. 309.
l. 22, *en . . . resnier*. *En* is generally followed by an inf. in this text. *Resnier* (for *raisnier*) may also mean *parler, discourir, plaider*.

30 Pour faire ses gens apaier;	In order to have his people satisfied;
La secunde, de franchement	The second, to reign sincerely
Regnier et sanz estorchement;	And without extortion;
De servitutes oster toutes	To remove all servitude
Et toutes autres males, toutes;	And all other evils, all;
35 La tierce, de largement vivre.	The third, to live generously.
Ce sunt les trois fins de leur livre,	Those are the three aims of their book,
Qui bonnes sunt et à plesir;	Which are good and pleasing;
Si les doit-on lire à lesir;	So, one should read them at leisure;
Et ce doivent faire touz princes,	And this should all princes do,
40 Qui à gouverner ont provinces.	Who have provinces to govern.
Mes encor autre chose y faut,	But still another thing is needed there,
De quoy il firent un deffaut;	Of which they made an omission;
Quar en leur ditez touché point	For in their "dits" they have not touched at all
N'ont de leur necessaire point,	On their necessary point,—
45 Et gouverner sagement.	And on governing wisely.
L'Escriture dit,—qui ne ment,—	The Scripture,—which does not lie,—says
Que touz Roys par la sapience	That all Kings by wisdom
Regnent partout; c'est la sentence	Should reign everywhere; that is the decree
Salemont et le jugement;	And the judgment of Solomon;
50 Nul ne doit regnier autrement.	No one should reign otherwise.
Ce noble point sauve leur grace:	This noble point is the saving grace for them [the poets]:
Mirent en leur diz en espasce,	They meditate upon their "dits,"
Qui ne fait pas à oublier;	Which meditation makes them not forget;
Quer touz autres poinz fait lier.	For this point causes all others to be linked together.
55 Le point, qui n'est lié en table,	The point which is not linked in a table
Seür n'est pas, ferme, n'estable;	Is not sure, firm, nor stable;
Mes par pou de poinz sera prins,	But it will be ensnared by a small number of points.
Se(Ce) je sai, quar je l'ai aprins;	This I know, for I have learned it;
Mes le lié ne doute point	But the linked [point] does not fear
60 Hazart, pointure, ne point.	Hazard, nor damage, nor [other] point.
Sur les clers aussi trop parlerent;	Also they talked too much about the clerics;
Le droit chemin pas n'i alerent,	They did not pursue there the straight road,
Et de Sainte Eglise ont dité	And about Holy Church they have written

l. 40 Cf. l. 771 and *La Comète*, l. 130.
l. 49. See ll. 812 ff. for a longer discussion of Solomon.
ll. 51-60. The "point" which is foremost in the author's mind is that of l. 45: "gouverner sagement".
l. 52, *Mirent . . . en espasce*, look in space. Cf. l. 29 of *Du Roy Phelippe*.

	Aucunne chose en leur dité	Something in their "dit,"
65	Qu'i[l] ne deüssent pas avoir dit,—	Which they should not have said, —
	Le dit qui conseille à descroitre	The "dit" which counsels to diminish
	Sainte Eglise que l'en deüst crostre;	Holy Church, which should be increased;
	Peché seroit tollir son droit;	It would be a sin to remove her right
	Si faillirent en cel endroit.	So, they failed in this place.
70	Pour ce, ai-ge un dit apres ci fait,	Wherefore, I have composed a "dit" hereinafter,
	Par cui peut estre manifait	By which it can be manifest
	Qu'i[l] ne furent pas bien meniers	That they were not very clever
	En ces trois poinz diz dureniers;	In these three points last mentioned;
	Si en dirai par mon avis	So, I shall say through my wisdom
75	C'en que bien m'en sera avis,	That wherein will indeed be my opinion about them,
	Non pas pour autrui mestrier,	Not in order to dominate others,
	Mes pource que veil destrier	But because I wish to place
	C'en qu'est de bon entendement	That wherein there is good understanding
	De c'en où faut amendement.	To the right of that wherein amending is needed.
80	Il n'est nul qui bien ne folie	There is no one who does not indeed go astray
	En icelle melencolie.	In that sorry frame of mind.
	Touz ne sont pas bien avisé;	All are not well advised;
	Dit mout souventes foiz,—Pis!—é(ai),	I have very oftentimes said, "Worse!"
	Y a plus loing *autré(outré)* ne qu'erré.	There is greater exaggeration therein than error.
85	Et s'autre ou moy a meserré,	And if another or I have erred,
	Ne nous devons pas courrouser,	We should not become angry,
	De cuer ne de bouche groucer	Nor scold in heart or in speech
	A ceus qui amendé aront	At those who will have amended
	C'en qu'en noz diz maudit *saront* (*s'aront*).	That wherein in our "dits" they will have censured thus.
90	Pour ce, pri que mon dit l'en voie,	Wherefore, I pray that my "dit" be examined,
	Et se de voir riens se desvoie,	That if anything wanders from the truth,

l. 65, *dit*. The scribe probably omitted a verse after l. 65, since there is no rhyme for *dit*.
l. 72, *meniers*, for *maniers*.
l. 77, *destrier*, for *destrer*, to accompany, to be to the right of.
l. 83. Other possible readings: *Dit m'ont souventes foiz, Pis! (h)é, They have oftentimes said to me, "Worse!*

Well, . . .; Pis e(st) (with an exaggerated effort to get rhyme for the eye), "*It is worse.*" Cf. *dit é*, in line 217.
l. 84, literally: *There is farther exaggerated therein than erred.*
l. 89, *saront* might also be corrected to *sarons*, and the verse translated: *That for which . . . we shall be censured.*

Encor à touz quier et pri-ge	Again I beg and pray all
Qu'en charité l'en le corrige:	That in charity it be corrected:
L'un à l'autre faire le doit,	One ought to do so for another,
95 Et pour ce, en lieve mon doit.	And for this reason, may my debit be removed.
Aussi com trop grater peut cuire,	Just as too much scratching may destroy (burn),
Aussi le trop parler peut nuire.	So, too much speaking may injure.
Pour ce, dit celui qui ne ment	Wherefore, he who does not lie says
Qu'en doit parler meiennement;	That people should speak in a middle-course manner (moderately);
100 Quer la parolle fait connoistre	For the speech makes known
D'omme l'estat et tout son estre;	The state of man and all his being;
Et qui si sa parolle part	And he who thus distributes his words
A droit, sanz pendre nulle part,	Rightly, without inclining anywhere,
Ne à destre ne à senestre,	Either to the right or to the left,
105 De bon temps pout *ou(au)* monde nestre.	Could have been born to the world in good season.
Aucuns ne l'ont pas bien parti	Some have not distributed them well,
Qui de mesure sont parti,	Who have departed from measure,
Qu'en doit bien tenir pour alain.	Which should indeed be regarded as a standard measure,
Et cuiderent pescher à l'ain,	And they thought to fish with a hook,
110 Mes leur ain estoit trop apart;	But their hook was too apparent;
Mau se cuevre qui derrier part.	Poorly covers himself he who leaves last.
Leur bouche, qu'il ont trop ouvert,	Their mouths, which they have opened too far,
Ha leur cuer dedens descouvert.	Have uncovered what is within their hearts.
Uns hons une rime fait a,	A man made a rhyme,
115 Que de parler bel afaita,	Which he arranged beautifully to recite,
Mes riens n'i vaut l'afaitement;	But the arrangement is worth nothing;
Si vous dirai comfaitement:	And I shall tell you why:
Quar oustre mesure est passez,	For beyond measure he passed,
Et trop parla. Non pas assez,	And he spoke too much. Not enough,
120 Non pas, pourtant, assez de bien	Not, however, enough good things
Dit a; et mout enseigne bien	Did he say; and very well he teaches
Au Roy de largesse tenir,	The King to maintain generosity,
Et son roiaume franc maintenir,	And to keep his realm free,
En son dité tout environ;	All around in his "dit";
125 Mes trop bouta son aviron	But too far did he put his oar
Outre mesure en la mer.	Beyond measure into the sea.
Adonques li creva la mer,	Then the sea burst upon him,

l. 95, *doit*, here has the force of *errors*.
ll. 96-7. The same idea is found in *La Comète*, ll. 209-10, in reverse order.
l. 108, *alain*, for *alaine*, agrarian measure.

Et soy-meïsmes contredit	And he contradicted himself
En c'en que *ou(au)* dité dit	In that wherein in the "dit" he says
130 Qu'en ne devroit à autrui faire,	That one should not do to another
Qu'en ne voudroit de lui, affaire;	An action which one would not wish from him;
Et il le fist, quant sus clergié	And he did so, when about the clergy
Parla trop, dont il est chergié;	He spoke too much, by which [superfluity] he is overburdened;
Et quant de son voisin mau dit,	And when he speaks ill of his neighbor,
135 Je di que ce n'est nul beau dit.	I say that this is not a beautiful "dit."
Pour ce, son dité tien-ge vain,	Wherefore, I regard his "dit" vain,
Quar trop y a mis de levain,	For he has put therein too much leaven,
Que le remenant corrumpu	Which the rest of his "dit"
De son dité a et rumpu.	Has corrupted and broken up.
140 Les clers ne tient pas à amis,	He does not consider the clerics as friends,
Pour ce, tant levain y a mis.	For that reason, did he put so much leaven therein.
Et se bien son[t] dit espion,	And if indeed they are called spies,
Il resemble à l'escorpion,	He resembles the scorpion,
Qui au premier oint et puis point.	Which at first anoints and then stings.
145 Aussi fait-il, et en ce point	So, does he, and in this point
Encor, qui bien son dit recorde,	Also, which well sums up his "dit,"
Aus .ii. bouz le milieu descorde,	The middle is discordant with the two ends,
Qui miex j[a] deüst concorder.	Which ought indeed to have harmonized better.
Pour ce, ne doit-on recorder	Wherefore, no "'dit" should be related
150 Nul dité, dont l'en peut retraire	Whereof it may be said
Que fins et milliéu sont contraire.	That the ends and middle are of contrary ideas (in contradiction).
Ne pas, pour tant, le bon eslire	Not, however, should one select the good,
Doit-on, et mettre en tirelire.	And put it in a jingle.
De cuer l'en doit essaier	Whole-heartedly one should try
155 Le bien prendre, le mal saier,—	To take the good, to test the evil,—
Saier et retrencher et rompre,—	To test and cut out and break it off,—
Qu'i[l] ne puisse le bien corrumpre.	So that it may not be able to corrupt the good.
Seignour, l'en doit par un mestrait	Lord, one is under obligations through a trickery
Que un home à son jeu mestrait;	That a man commits at his game;
160 Que son jeu en part, nul n'en doute;	That his game starts therefrom, no one doubts;

l. 133, *dont il est chergié*, may also mean *with whom (=clergié) he is entrusted*. Perhaps also the idea is that the poet was *chargé* (commanded) to write on the clergy.

l. 144, *oint et . . . point*. Cf. *Un Songe*, ll. 356-7.
l. 160, *part*, may also be read: *pait*, *feeds*.

Aussi font maintes genz sanz doute.	So, do many people act without doubt.
Et ce *que(qui)* d'eux bien dit sera,	And what good will be said of them,
Pour pou de chose versera.	For very little, will be reversed.
Chascun de tiex la vache semble,	Each one of such people resembles the cow,
165 Qui, son lait trait et mis ensemble,	Which, its milk drawn and put together [in one pail],
Son pie estent, qu'il en meschiet,	Extends its foot, so that misfortune comes therefrom:
Que le pot brise et le lait chiet.	The pot breaks and the milk is spilt.
Ainsi aucune gent ont fait	Thus some people have done
En aucuns ditez qui sont fait.	In some "dits" which are composed.
170 Je ne sai comment ont posé	I do not know how they have placed
Leur cuer à ce que proposé	Their hearts, so that they may have made statements
Aient ainsi contre clergié.	Thus against the clergy.
Chascun en a s'ame chargié,	Each has burdened his soul therewith,
Mes le venin, qu'au cuer avoient	But the poison, which they had in their hearts
175 Contre clergié, pas ne savoient	Against the clergy, they did not know
Comment hors le pouïssent mettre.	How they might put it out.
Pour ce, *ce(se)* voudrent entremettre	Wherefore, they wished to busy themselves
Contre eux de rime desploier,—	With deploying rhyme against them,—
Bien cuident leur temps emploier,—	They think they are well employing their time,—
180 Et desenfler leur cuers cuiderent,	And they thought to remove the swelling from their hearts,
Quant de ce venin le vuiderent,	When they emptied them of this poison,
Qu'orent contre clers conceü;	Which they had conceived against clerics.
Mes en cuidant sont deceü;	But in such thinking they are deceived;
Ne soi-meïsmes pas n'amerent,	Nor did they love themselves,
185 Ainsois leur estat diffamerent.	Rather did they defame their position.
Et ont au Roy amonesté	And they have exhorted the King
Tel chose qui n'est d'onesté,	To such action which is not honest,
Comme de boire et de mengier,	As in regard to drinking and eating,
Dont à court ont eu dangier,	Whereof at court they have had control,
190 Et d'assez de choses semblab[l]es,	And a number of similar things,
Que l'en doit tenir com pour fables.	Which should be regarded as idle talk.

l. 163, *versera*, may be translated: *change, be overturned*.
l. 167, *chiet*, literally *falls*.
l. 173, *s'ame*, may also be read: *s'aine*, *his hatred*.
l. 189, *à court*, may also mean: *for a short time*.

Quar il dient leur vilenie,	For they say their vileness,
Quant plus pensent de gloutonie,	When most they think of gluttony,
Quant à parler vilainnement,	When in speaking vilely,
195 Qui ne sont du gouvernement,	They who are not of the government,
Moustrer(moustrent) au Roy, qui ores regne,	Show the King, who now reigns,
Comment doit gouverner son regne.	How he should govern his kingdom.
A ceci ne sont pas bien entre,	For this they are certainly not within;
Ençois plus pensent de leur ventre,	Rather more do they think of their stomachs,
200 Et de l'argent le Roy avoir.	And of having the money of the King.
Qui ne sunt en sens, n'en savoir,	They who are not in their senses, nor in knowledge,
En leur dité demandent gages.	In their "dit" ask for wages.
Je ne sai se rien ont en (en)gages,	I do not know if they have anything in pledges,
Que il voussissent racheter,	That they might wish to redeem,
205 Ou s'il veulent riens acheter	Or if they wish to buy things
De l'avoir au Roy qu'il demandent.	With the wealth of the King which they ask for.
En ce leurs ditéz pas n'amendent.	In this they do not amend their "dits."
Ne pour tant, se le Roy monnoie	Nevertheless, if the King owes them money,
Leur doit, droiz est qu'i[l] les en oie.	It is right that he hear them thereon.
210 Se le Roy ont en rien servi,	If they have in anything served the King,
Que du sien aient deservi,	So that they may have merited some of his wealth,
Trop comperent en demander.	Too much do they acquire in asking.
Pour ce, doit le Roy commander	Wherefore, the King should command
Que du leur riens en ne retieingne.	That naught be held back of theirs.
215 Ainsinc est droiz que l'en se tieigne.	It is right that one conduct himself thus.
Et je croi que de leur dité	And I believe that the intention
Est l'entention que dit *é(ai)*.	Of their "dit" is as I have said.
Si n'en veil nul d'eux accuser,	So, I do not wish to accuse any of them,
Mes par nulle chose escuser	But by nothing can they
220 Ne se pevent-il en leurs rimes,	Excuse themselves in their rhymes,
Où l'en voit manifestez crimes.	Wherein manifest crimes are seen.

l. 196, *Roy, qui ores regne.* Cf. title of the third poem.
l. 198, *entre,* appears to be used as an adverb of place. The p. p. *entré* might give a better meaning, but the meter requires the verse to end in a mute *e*.
l. 200, *le Roy,* gen. case.
l. 203, *(en)gages.* This verse has an extra syllable. The second *en* seems to be the unnecessary syllable.
l. 217, *ê(ai).* Cf. l. 83.

Quant de la juridiction	When about the jurisdiction of the Church
Font de l'Eglise à diction,	They make statements
En son grief, en son prejudice,	To her grief, to her prejudice,
225 Chascun se merveille d'ice.	Every one is astounded thereby.
Il dirent bien qu'or n'ont mes rien,	They indeed said that now they no longer get anything,
Quer il ne sunt pas du merrien	For they are not of the type
Aus clers, n'ausi de leur partie.	Of the clerics, nor of their party either.
La chose d'eux est mal partie.	The matter is badly started by them.
230 Aucuns de ceus, pour leurs meffez,	Some of these, for their misdeeds,
Ont deservi d'estre deffez;	Have deserved to be undone;
Enquor feüssent ce-ce veire:	Although these [sayings] might be the truth:
Que l'Eglise est trop debonnaire,	That the Church is too good-natured,
Et touz jours endure et atent,	And always endures and waits,
235 Et atendra jusques à tant,—	And will wait until so long,—
Combien que l'aient *lesdengiée* *(desdengiée)*,	However much they may have disdained her,—
Qu'elle soit par autrui vengiée.	That she may be avenged by others.
Aucuns aussi achoisonné	Some also have been accused
Ont esté et enprisonné;	And imprisoned;
240 Ne de ce n'ont eu respit.	Nor from this have they had respite.
Pource que fait orent despit	Because they had caused vexation
A Sainte Eglise sanz raison,	To Holy Church without reason,
Ce fu droit, non pas desraison.	This was right, not unreasonableness.
En leurs ditez un pou en touchent,	In their "dits" they speak thereof a little,
245 Mes jusques au vif n'i atouchent.	But they do not go clear to the vital point.
Si n'en font pas bien leur devoir,	So, they do not well their duty,
Quant il n'en dient tout de voir.	When they tell not all the truth thereon.
Il ne peut pas estre nié	It cannot be denied
Qu'aucun d'eus escommenié	That some of them are not excommunicated therefor.
250 N'en soient. Voirs en est commune,	Truly, it is a common thing,—
Par plusieurs foiz, non pas par une.	Several times, not once.
Pour ce, l'Eglise en ont haïe.	Wherefore, they have hated the Church.
Qu'en fera-elle? Dex aïe!	What will she do about that? May God help!
Seront, pour ce, clers mis en mue?	Will clerics, for this, be put in confinement?

l. 226, *mes,* for *mais, more.*
l. 227, *merrien,* for *mairien, wood for construction; nature, kind.*

l. 233, *que,* may be for *quer, for.*
l. 254, *mue,* also: *place of retreat, hiding-place.*

255 Nennil! Quar droit ne se remue,	Not at all! For rightly she does not bestir herself,
S'ensemble à ceste fin s'alient;	If they ally themselves together for this purpose;
Quer Sainte Eglise contralient.	For they torment Holy Church.
L'Eglise ne s'esmoie en ce;	The Church is not troubled thereby;
Touz jours vaincra par pacience.	She will always conquer by patience.
260 Et *si(se)* la vuellent guerroier,	And if they wish to make war on her,
Et son droit taillier et roier,	And cut and snatch away her right,
Bien en pourront, en lieu de don,	Well may they have, in place of gift,
Avoir un autel guerredon,	Such a reward,
Com ot le peuple de Mahom	As had the people of Mohammed
265 En ce temps du Roy Pharaon,	In the time of the King Pharaoh,
Qui les Juys vouloit estaindre.	Who wished to extinguish the Jews.
Pour ce, les voult Dieu touz ataindre	Wherefore, God wished to overtake them all
Dedenz la mer, où il naierent.	In the sea, where they drowned.
Nonques lors nuls n'en eschaperent.	Never, then, did any one of them escape.
270 En celle ancienne figure	In this ancient personage
L'Escript nous demoustre et figure	The Scripture demonstrates and portrays for us
Comme seront encor punis	How will be punished again
Ceus qui sont ensemble unis	Those who are united together
Pour l'Eglise desheriter.	To disinherit the Church.
275 Contre Dieu ne peut nul liter.	Against God no one can struggle.
S'aucun contre l'Eglise tence,	If some one disputes against the Church,
Et elle punit par sentence,	And she punishes by judgment,
Elle fait comme malgré lui.	She acts as if in spite of herself.
Dira-il, pour ce, mal de lui?	Will he, for this reason, say evil about her?
280 Quant la correcion n'a pris,	When he has not taken the correction,
De son malves cuer n'a apris;	He has not learned with his evil heart;
Et pour ce, nous a mains valu	And for this reason, the correction has been of less value
Le corrigement à salu.	To us for salvation.
N'en autre guise eus vengier	Nor in other guise do they know how
285 Ne se sevent qu'en lo sengier.	To avenge themselves except in dreaming.
Il ont hui tort et plus tort hier.	They are wrong today and more wrong yesterday.
Touz jours sent les auz le mortier.	Always does the mortar smell of garlic.
Nequedant de touz entechiez	Nevertheless, of all positions
Estaz en a de granz pechiez,	There are some possessed of great sins,
290 Et se maintiennent ordement.	And they maintain themselves ignobly.

l. 257, *contralient* also: *contradict, oppose*.

l. 262, *roier*, for *raier*.
ll. 264 ff. Cf. *Exodus*, XIV.

Ne n'en finit nul amendement,	Nor does any of them complete improvement,
N'à Dieu ne veulent reperer.	Nor do they wish to make amends to God.
En ce, n'a rien à comperer	In this, the Church has naught to pay for,
L'Eglise, qui, de son office,	Which, by her service,
295 Euvre contre la malefice.	Works against misdeed.
Encor font-il plus à reprendre,	Still do they more to be reproved,
Quant il veullent le Roy aprendre	When they wish to inform the King
Que l'Eglise ne lesse à croistre;	That he not allow the Church to increase;
Mes li vuellent faire descroistre	But they wish to make decrease for her
300 Ce qu'a aquis temporelment.	What she has acquired temporally.
En ce, parlent trop cruelment	In this, they speak too cruelly
Contre Sainte Eglise, leur mere.	Against Holy Church, their mother.
Ceste parolle est trop amere,	This word is too bitter,
Et trop poingnant et trop aguë,	And too poignant and too sharp,
305 Qui si contre sa mere arguë.	Which argues thus against one's mother.
Les fis qui n'aiment leur parenz,—	Sons who love not their parents,—
Selonc les Escrips apparenz,—	According to the clear Scriptures,—
Ou charnés ou esperités,	Either carnal or spiritual,
Puis qu'à leur mere sunt ytés,	Since they are such to their mother,
310 Bonne fin ne pevent ensuivre.	Cannot carry out a good end.
Ne l'en ne les doit lessier vivre,	They should not be let to live,
Quar mortel li sont anemi.	For they are mortal enemies to her.
L'acort font de fa et de mi	They make the chord of the notes *fa* and *mi* [discord]
Par leur langue, qui point et trenche,	By their tongue, which stings and cuts,
315 Et conseille au Roy qu'i[l] retrenche	And counsels the King that he cut off
Sainte Eglise. C'est male pointe:	Holy Church. That is an evil sting:
Touz jours brait la roe male ointe.	The poorly oiled wheel squeaks always.
Roys, conseillier l'en te deüt	King, they should have counseled thee
Que Sainte Eglise s'acreüt,	That Holy Church be increased,
320 Et qu'à lui n'eüsses *comteps(contemps)*;	And that thou shouldst not have quarrel with her;
Mes li feïsses en touz temps	But that thou shouldst do for her at all times
Ce que tes devanciers li firent.	What thy predecessors did for her.
Onques en riens ne li forfirent,	Never in anything did they harm to her,
Et pour ce, ont-il eu entrées	And for this reason, have they had entry

ll. 306-10. Cf. *Exodus* 20: 12 and *Ephesians* 6: 1-3.

1. 320, *contemps*, may also mean: *scorn*, but cf. *Un Songe*, l. 210.

325 Par les paÿs, par les contrées,	Through the countries, through the lands.
Et seür leur anemis victoires;	And victories over their enemies;
Si com racontent les histoires.	Just as the histories relate.
De ce, font-il bien mencion,	Of this, they indeed make mention,
Mes en ce, ont male entention,	But in that, evil intention have they
330 Qui dient c'onques(qu'onques) ceus n'userent	Who say that never did these make use
De conseil de clers; lors ruserent,	Of counsel of clerics; then they used deceit,
Et en ce dire ont-il mestrait.	And in saying this they have tricked.
Touz jours les clers, au plus estrait	Always the clerics, for the most intimate
Conseil des Réaus, ont esté	Counsel of Royalties, have been
335 Par devers la court aresté.	Detained in the presence of the court.
Roys, deffen l'Eglise et gouverne,	King, defend the Church and govern,
Ne li fai pas fourches de verne.	Make not alder forks for her.
Touz ceus qui li ont foy tenue,	All those who have kept faith with her,
Et acreüe et maintenue,	And increased and maintained her,
340 Ont eu la prosperité,	Have had prosperity,
La victoire et l'auctorité,	Victory and authority,
Touz jours, de semaine en semaine.	Always, from week to week.
Bien parut au grant Challemaine,	Well did it appear to great Charlemagne,
Qui tant de terres mist à plain,	Who laid low so many lands,
345 Et partout fu sires à plain,	And everywhere was complete master,
Et parfit quanqu'il entama;	And carried out all that he started;
Pource que Sainte Eglise ama.	Because he loved Holy Church.
En ce, son temps bien emploia;	In that, he well employed his time;
Par lui moult se mouteplia	Through him Holy Church greatly enriched herself,
350 Sainte Eglise, et moult y aquit	And acquired much thereby,
Qu'encores tient franc et aquit.	Which she still holds free and redeemed.
Pource que vers lui ne mesprist,	Because towards her he did not do wrong,
Le grant Rois tante terre prist.	The great King took so much land.
De Dieu prist et à Dieu donna;	From God he took and to God he gave;
355 A Sainte Eglise abandonna	To Holy Church he granted
Une tel grace et privilege	Such favor and privilege
Que chascun evesque en son sege	That each bishop in his see
Et en son leu ait connoissance	And in his place should have knowledge
Vers touz et en touz cas puissance,	About all, and in all cases power,
360 Et d'oïr et d'examiner,	Both to hear and to examine,
Et par sentence terminer,	And to terminate by judgment,
Sans apel et sans contredit.	Without appeal and without contradiction.

1. 337, *fourches de verne*, figurative for *forced labor*.

Le droit ancien si le dit,	The ancient law thus states,
Si com je l'ai dit orendroit,	Just as I have said now,
365 Aussi fait le decret en droit,	Also does the decree in law,
Clerement comme une lumiere,	Clearly as a light,
En celle question premiere	In this first question
De l'onzieme cause, en canon,	Of the eleventh case, in canon law,
Quicunquez le chapitre a non.	Whatever name the chapter has.
370 Puis cestui Charlle Emperëour,—	Then, this Charles, the Emperor,—
Et Roy ne fu de li mëour,	And there was not a King better than he,
Ne qui tant redouté feüst,	Nor who might be so feared,
Ne qui tant de richesse eüst,—	Nor who might have so much wealth,—
Et qui autre si com li furent,	And others who thus were like him,
375 Et touz jours prosperité urent,	And always had prosperity,
Touz leurs fais pourent achever,	Were able to complete all their acts,
N'en riens pourent meschever.	Nor could they fail in anything.
Et,— que ne me soit reprouvé,—	And,—lest I be reproved,—
Par plusieurs princes est prouvé	It is proved by several princes
380 En Viez et Nouviau Testament,	In Old and New Testaments,
Et d'autre part, se Dex m'ament,	And elsewhere,— if God belies me,—
Par les histoires de jadis,	By the histories of former times,
Dont toust conteroie-j[e] adiz.	Whereof I, summoned, would quickly relate.
Prouveroit-on ce que vous conte,	What I say to you would be proved
385 Qui bien vous en diroit le conte.	By him who would truly tell you the story thereof.
Constentin, le grant Emperiere,	Constantine, the great Emperor,
Celui qui fu ça en arriere,	The one who lived some time ago,
Ne donna-il le patremoine,	Did he not give the patrimony,
En proprieté, en demoine,—	In property, in domain,—
390 Le patremoine de Saint Pere?	The patrimony of Holy Father?
Encor en usent li Saint Pere,	Still do the Holy Fathers use it,
Et en sont en possession;	And are in possession of it;
Nonques n'en firent cession.	They never relinquished it.
Et puis qu'i[l] fu consilié	And since he was reconciled
395 A Sainte Eglise et alié,	And allied to Holy Church,
Nus homs ne le pout contrester;	No man could stand against him;
Tant li donna Dex conquester,—	So much did God give him to conquer,—
Chastiaux et citez, villes, bours,—	Castles and strongholds, cities, towns,—
Que ses anemis à rebours	That he put all his enemies back
400 Mist touz et à destruction.	And to destruction.
Contre lui n'orent action.	Against him they had not battle.
Sainte Eglise n'oublia mie;	Holy Church he did not forget at all;
Pour ce, touz jourz li fu amie.	Wherefore, she was always friendly to him.

1. 381, *m'ament*, may also read: *n'i ament, does not lie therein.*

En ceste maniere et par tel	In this manner and by such
405 Fait tant conquist au martel,	Action he conquered so much with the hammer,
Et touz et chascun martela,	And hammered each and every one,
Qui contre li se revela.	Who revealed himself against him.
Batailles vainqui et assaus,	Battles and assaults he won,
Et par Sainte Eglise fu saus.	And through Holy Church he was safe.
410 Aussi fu le Roy Dagoubert:	Also there was the King Dagobert:
Ne pour lance, ne pour haubert,	Not for lance, not for hauberk,
Seulement, n'ot-il pas aquis,	Only, had he acquired,
Ce qu'en France tu tiens aquis,	What in France thou holdest acquired,
Et en sa vie et puis apres,	Both in his life and then afterwards,
415 Se l'Eglise ne li fust pres.	If the Church had not been near to him.
Vaincu et dampné eüt esté,	Conquered and subdued he would have been,
Mes aussi anemi contresté	But also an enemy opposed
Ens Saint Denis et Saint Morise,	By Saint Denis and Saint Maurice,
Si com l'istoire nous devise.	Just as history relates to us.
420 Ainsi s'eschapa-il des cous,	Thus he escaped from the blows,
Et des dyables fu rescous	And from the devils he was rescued
Par l'Eglise, qui à bon sert.	By the Church, which serves for good.
Par droit bon loier en desert.	By righteousness one deserves a good reward.
Aussi fu Theodosius,	Also there was Theodosius,
425 Non pas Pilatus Pocius.	Not Pontius Pilate.
Saint Loÿs aussi, qui fu Rois,	Saint Louis also, who was King,
Il ne fist contemps, ne desrois	He did not cause quarrel, nor disorder
Sainte Eglise, mes li maintint.	For Holy Church, but maintained her.
Pour ce, empès son réaume tint;	Wherefore, in peace he held his realm;
430 Et si n'ot de nulle part guerre;	And so, he had not war from any side;
Et du sien voust .ii. foiz requerre	And with his people he wished twice to seek out
Nostre Seigneur outre la mer.	Our Lord, beyond the sea.
Saint Loÿs en lui n'ot amer.	Saint Louis had not bitterness in him.
De lui, Roys, es-tu estraiz;	From him, King, thou are descended;
435 Sages es, s'à lui te retraiz;	Wise art thou, if thou resemblest him;
Et de lui portes-tu le non.	And from him thou bearest thy name.
Or fai qu'aies autel renon,	Now act that thou mayest have like renown,
Si auras-tu, s'aimes l'Eglise.	So thou shalt have, if thou lovest the Church.
Ne croi pas homme qui te lise	Believe not any man who may read to thee
440 D'autre chose que je te di,	Other thing than I tell thee,

l. 416, *dampné*, also: damned.
l. 418, *ens*, literally: in.

l. 427, *contemps*, also *scorn*. Cf. l. 320.
l. 428, *Sainte Eglise*, dat. case.

Mes li respon et contredi,	But answer and contradict him,
Quar c'est mauvès esperit d'envie.	For that is the evil spirit of envy.
Se bonnement veus estre en vie,	If thou wishest to be kindly in life,
Croi l'Eglise, bonne gent monde.	Believe the Church,—a kind, pure people.
445 Se vivre veus empès au monde,	If thou wishest to live in peace in the world,
Ne croi pas chascun qui parolle.	Believe not every one who speaks.
Pensse le droit en la parolle	Think what is right in the word
De chascun qui rens te dira;	Of every one who will say things to thee;
Entent où leur pensée ira,—	Understand where their thought will lead,—
450 De ceus qui conseillent destruire	Of those who counsel to destroy
Sainte Eglise, que doiz construire.	Holy Church, which thou shouldst construct.
Roys, oste-toi de tout effroi,	King, remove thyself from all fright,
Pense à Conradin et Mainfroi	Think of Conradin and Manfred
Et Federi, comment morurent,	And Frederick, how they died,
455 Pour ce que l'Eglise coururent;	Because they pursued the Church;
Pour leurs gries et pour leur torfais	For their pains and for their misdeeds
Honteusement furent mors fais.	In shame were they put to death.
Hé! Roys Loÿs, pensse à ton pere!	Ah! King Louis, think of thy father!
Je dout que aussi ne compere	I fear that also he may not merit
460 Les guetes qui ont esté faites,	The watches which have been made,
S'à point ne les mes et à faites.	If thou dost not put them in condition and to completion.
Se l'Eglise eüst empès tenu,	If he had kept the Church in peace,
Tant de maus ne fussent venu	So many ills would not have come
En son temps, com il[en]avint.	In his time, as there occurred.
465 Par Sainte Eglise cela vint,	By Holy Church that came about,
Qui pour lui de cuer ne prioit,	Which for him did not pray from her heart,
Pource que trop fort la prioit.	Because he begged her too strongly.
Or pensses, Roys, regarde et voies,	Now think, King, look and see,
Quar, se tu tout le monde avoies,	For, if thou hadst all the world,
470 Et l'Eglise tant seulement	And the Church only
Feüst contre toi, nullement	Were against thee, not at all
Ne pourroies-tu endurer,	Wouldst thou be able to endure,
N'à longues, n'à la fin durer.	Nor to last long, nor to the end.
De Dieu vient et victoire et force,	From God comes both victory and strength,
475 Si est fol qui contre lui force.	So, foolish is he who strives against Him.

l. 444, *bonne gent monde*, also: *she purifies kind people.*
l. 459, *compere*, may be for *comperes, thou mayest merit. Comperer*, also means *buy, acquire, pay for, expiate.*
l. 460, *guetes*, also: *watch-towers.*

l. 461, *à point . . . mes*, also: *adjust, conciliate, apease.*
l. 464, [en] is necessary for the meter.
l. 475, *lui*, may also refer to *Church*, since *lui* is sometimes fem. Cf. ll. 278-9.

Pense à Godefroi de Buillon,	Think of Godfrey of Bouillon,
Qui mal à l'Eglise aguillon	Who at first was an evil goad
Fu au premier et li meffit;	To the Church and did evil to her;
Et pour ce, outremer riens ne fist,	And for this reason, he did naught overseas,
480 Adont en ost, ne en bataille,	Then in campaign, nor in battle,
Pource que pris ot sus la taille;	Because he had taken above the poll-tax;
Et quant ce vit, si s'en tourna,	And when he saw this, he turned therefrom,
Et du tout rendre s'atourna.	And arranged to return everything.
Et lors prist-il la terre toute,	And then he took all the land,
485 Quant il ne fist taille, ne toute.	When he did not levy poll-tax, nor assessment.
Hé! Roys, nostre Seigneur ha point	Ah! King, our Lord has stung
Ton réaume: Pource qu'à point	Thy realm: Because Holy Church
N'a Sainte Eglise gouvernée	Has not been governed opportunely
Esté par gent malordenée,	By imprudent people,
490 Li sunt venuz touz ces esclandres;	All these scandals have come to it;
Or aus Anglois, et puis en Flandres	Now to the English, and later in Flanders
Sus apostolles, sus les Roys,	Upon apostles, upon Kings,
Et sus Roynes les desrois,—	And upon Queens the disorders [have come],—
Hommes, fames, en clers, en lais,	Men, women, among clerics, among laymen,
495 De touz les estaz, nus n'en lais,	Of all positions,— I do not omit any
Qui triboullé n'aient esté;	Who may not have been distressed;
Ce leur a fait leur mauvesté.	Their wickedness has done this to them.
Quar l'Eglise n'ont honnoré,	For they have not honored the Church,
Ne chiez eus n'a droit demouré;	Nor has righteousness dwelt among them;
500 Mes ceus qui l'Eglise exauciée	But those who have hearkened to the Church,
Ont, et foi et loi avanciée,	And advanced faith and law,
Ont eu victoire. Si feront	Have had victory. Thus will do
Touz ceuz qui loial li seront.	All those who will be loyal to her.
Ceste chose declert tout outre;	This thing explains everything else;
505 Viez et Nouvel Testament moutre,	The Old and New Testaments demonstrate [it],
Car, quant li Juif combatoient,	For, when the Jews were fighting,
Qui grant nombre de gent estoient,	Who were a numerous people,

l. 485, *toute* for *tolte*, which also means: *fine, theft, plunder.*
l. 486, *ha point*, may be *n'a point*, has not.
l. 490, *Li*, probably refers to *réaume* rather than to *Eglise.*

Quant Moÿses ses mains levoit	When Moses raised his hands in prayer,
En oroison, lors achevoit	Then the people achieved
510 Le peuple tout ce que vouloit,	All that they wished,
Et ses anemis defouloit.	And trampled their enemies.
Et quant ses mains jus abaissoit,	And when he lowered his hands,
La victoire adont leur cessoit.	Victory then ceased for them.
Pour ce, en Escrit est-il leü	For this reason, it is read in Scripture
515 Qu'aucuns estoient esleü,	That some were chosen,
Qui touz jourz ses mains soustenoient,	Who always held up his hands,
Quant Juys bataillier venoient.	When Jews came to fight.
Si estoient de toutes pars	So, in all directions
Leurs anemis mortels espars.	Their mortal enemies were scattered.
520 Roys, se tu veus que bien te viegne,	King, if thou wouldst have good come to thee,
Quier qui bien tes mains te sousteigne.	Seek her who will well hold up thy hands for thee.
Tant com l'Eglise levera	So long as the Church will raise
Ses mains et pour toy priera,	Her hands and pray for thee,
Tu vaincras et seürmonteras.	Thou shalt conquer and prevail.
525 De ce ja mal en douteras.	Wrongly indeed shalt thou doubt that.
Se l'Eglise pour toy ne prie,	If the Church does not pray for thee,
Roys, ne en France, ne en Brie,	King, neither in France, nor in Brie,
N'en terre de ta seignourie,	Nor in land of thy seigniory,
N'en force de chevalerie,	Nor in strength of knighthood,
530 N'ent(n'en) gent de pié, n'en forteresse,	Nor in foot-soldiers, nor in fortress,
Ne en amis, ne en richesse,	Nor in friends, nor in wealth,
Ne cuide pas que riens te vaillent;	Think not that anything may avail thee;
Mes chevaus au pié blanc faillent,	But horses with white feet fail,
Et l'Eglise à nullui ne faut,	And the Church fails no one,
535 Se de lui ne vient le defaut.	If the falling away from her occurs not.
Roys, contre l'Eglise ne bées,	King, gape not against the Church,
Mes fai comme les Machabées,	But do like the Maccabees,
Qui touz leur anemis vainquirent,	Who conquered all their enemies,
Et la bonne lai(loi) maintenirent.	And maintained the good law.
540 Comment Diex combatoit pour eus,	How God fought for them,
Il le veoient à leur eus;	They saw with their eyes;
Il proiaient, Diex combatoit,	They prayed, God fought,
Et leurs anemis abatoit.	And struck down their enemies.

ll. 508 ff. Cf. *Exodus* 17: 11, 12.
ll. 537 ff. The Maccabees led the Jews to victory over the Syrians. Story told in apocryphal *Books of Maccabees*.

Roy, fai tant qu'en ne te maudie,	King, act in such wise that no one may curse thee,
545 Et que chascuns de toy bien die,	And that every one speak well of thee,
Et pour toy prie. Lors aras	And pray for thee. Then thou shalt have
Tout ce que demander saras.	All that thou mayest ask for.
C'est verité, pas ne ment-on;	That is the truth, we do not lie:
Celi qui l'en tient le menton,	He who supports her,
550 Souef noe. Voi et esgarde	Tranquilly sails along. See and regard
Que se Dex ne te prent en garde,	That if God takes not care of thee,
Il n'est riens qui te puist garder.	There is naught which might guard thee.
Bien povez voir et regarder	Well mayest thou see and regard
Que pour toy nul de cuer prier	That for thee no one can pray earnestly,
555 Ne peut, se le veus *aprier(aprimer)*.	If thou wishest to overwhelm him.
S'en te conseille que tu toilles	If thou art advised to take
A l'Eglise et que la despoilles	From the Church and to despoil her of her own,—
Du sien,— ne sai en quel maniere,—	I know not in what manner,—
Elle feroit pour toy priere.	She would make prayer for thee.
560 Ce *ceroit(seroit)* priere de bouche,	That would be a prayer of the mouth,
Qui à douceur de cuer ne touche.	Which touches not gentleness of heart.
Hé! Roys, puis que tant est ton regne,	Well! King, since such is thy reign,
Aucune gent trop lache regne;	Some people, too cowardly, reign;
Si bonnement ont conseillié	So simply have they counseled
565 Que ton réaume en est essillié.	That thy realm is despoiled thereby.
Ce(Se) c'est par conseil de clergié,	If that is by advice of clergy,
Le deable les desfergie!	May the devil deliver them from the irons!
Ce ne sunt pas clers esprouvé,	They are not tested clerics,
Ainçois sunt faus et reprouvé,	Rather they are false and outcast,
570 Qui sunt pris par charnalité.	Who are seized by sensuality.
Es quiex n'a stabilité,	In such there is not stability,
Foy, léauté, ne couvenant;	Faith, loyalty, nor covenant;
Mes sunt le cochet à tout vent,	But they are the weathervane,
Qui de toutes parties clinent;	Who bow in all directions;
575 Par ainsi de France declinent	In this way they turn from France

l. 547, *saras*, literally: *will know how to*.
l. 549, *l'en tient le menton*, literally: *holds up her chin*.
l. 553, *povez*. The poet gains a syllable by using 2nd. per. plu.
l. 555, *aprimer*, fits the idea better than *aprier* (or *à prier*), *to beg* or *beseech*.
l. 565, *réaume en est essillié*, also may mean: *thy rule is driven out*.
l. 566, *Ce*. The MS. reading could be accepted: *That, that is by* ....
l. 574, *de toutes parties*, also: *to all projects*.

Bons estatuz, bons ordenemens,	Good statutes, good regulations,
Par les mauvès gouvernemens.	By bad governments.
Et ce de ceus vient,— c'est tout voir,—	And that comes from those,— this is quite true,—
Qui de la court font l'estouvoir;	Who do the necessary work of the court;
580 Et ces clers ont à la court mis,	And these clerics have put at the court,
Non pas les bons, mes leur amis,	Not the good men, but their friends,
Charneus, qui sunt de leur lignage,	Relatives, who are of their lineage,
Ou leurs voisins par voisignage,	Or their neighbors, through neighborliness.
Et se au réaume aucune greté	And if to the realm any suffering,
585 Ou aucun meschief a esté,	Or any misfortune, has happened,
Tiex maus sunt par tiex clers venuz.	Such ills have come through such clergy.
Se par clergié sunt avenuz,—	If through clergy they have happened,—
Non mie par clers de science	Not at all by clerics chosen from knowledge,
Esleüz, ou par prouvëence,—	Or by test,—
590 Si n'en doivent estre blasmé,	So, should not be blamed,
Vituperé, ne diffamé,	Vituperated, nor defamed,
Les bons, mes (mes) les mauvès comperent	The good men; but let the evil pay for
Les mauvestiez que(qui) par eus perent!	The wicked things which through them appear!
Onque puis que tel gent ancré	Ever since such people were anchored
595 Furent à court, ne exancré,	At court, and not set adrift,
N'a esté que guerre et meslée.	There has been only war and conflict.
Chascun en a pris sa pelée,	Each one has taken his shovelful,
Si en sunt les genz desnuées,	So, the people are stripped,
Et ou(au) réaume les guerres nées;	And in the realm wars born;
600 Le tien, Deus, eus porté ont.	Thine, God, they have carried off.
Qui une escorche, .ii. ne tont.	He who skins one, does not shear two.
De toy ont eu le bienfait,	From thee they have had their profit,
Mes au réaume n'ont riens bien fait.	But for the realm they have done nothing good.
Par itès clers les maus avienent,	Through such clerics do the ills arise,
605 Se par les clers au réaume vienent;	If by clerics they come to the realm;
Pour ce, conseil esleü tien,	For this reason, take select counsel (keep an appointed counsel),
Et vif desoremès du tien,	And living henceforth from thine own,

l. 582, *charneus*, also: *intimates*, or it may be an adj., *intimate*, modifying *amis*.
l. 592. *(mes)*. The scribe put in an extra *mes*.

l. 593, *perent*, from *paroir*.
l. 598, *desnuées* also: *abandoned*. The reading may also be: *desunées, disunited*.

Pren conseil *au(où)* prendre t'avises;	Take counsel where thou presumest to take [it];
Ne le pren pas par talantises,	Take it not through whims,
610 Mes eslis le grain de la paille;	But select the grain from the straw;
Se ton réaume veus que bien aille,	If thou wishest thy realm to go well,
Pren gent qui sachent droit et *lais(lois)*.	Take people who know the right and laws.
Tu ne peuz sanz clers et sanz lais:	Thou canst not do without clerics and laymen.
Les sages clers pour conseillier,	The wise clerics to advise,
615 Chevaliers, lais pour bataillier,	Knights, laymen to do battle,
Un et autre sunt necessaire,	Both are necessary,
L'un, principal; l'autre, acessaire.	The one, principal; the other, accessory.
Du tans de l'ancianeté	From the time of antiquity
Touz jours ainsiques a eté	Always has it been thus
620 Que la bonne chevalerie	That good knighthood
Suit, et auxi la clergie.	Ensues, and also clergy.
Roys, merveillès ne t'en demaines:	King, trouble not thyself excessively about it:
Ne fut au premier à Atheinnes	Was not first at Athens
La clergie et la sapience?	The clergy (scholars) and wisdom?
625 Et la chevalerie en ce	And the knighthood at this point
Point tantoust à Atheines vint.	Presently came to Athens.
Et quant clergie partir convint	And when clergy agreed to set out
De Athaines pour Troie destruite,	From Athens for the destruction of Troy,
Bien tost après s'en est fuite	Very soon afterwards hastened thence
630 Chevalerie après clergié.	Knighthood after clergy.
Après ce, furent hebergié	After this, there were lodged
Sapience et clers à Romme,	At Rome wisdom and clerics,
Et après, tost le gentil homme.	And soon afterwards the noble men.
Les chevaliers tant y suïrent	The knights, in such numbers, followed there
635 Qu'à Romme les clers consuïrent.	That at Rome they overtook the clerics.
Et grant temps y ont demouré,	And a long time they stayed there,
Dont le païs fu honnouré.	By which the country was honored.
Et tant com demourant y furent,	And so long as they were staying there,
Les Rommains partout puissance urent.	The Romans everywhere had power.
640 Mes de la maniere diray	But in that manner I shall tell
Le voir, ne ja ne mentiray.	The truth, nor now shall I lie.
Li sage clerc si conseilloient,	The wise clerics thus counseled
Et li chevalier batailloient.	And the knights battled.
Par ce qui estoit conseillé,	By what was advised,

l. 610. Cf. *Desputoison*, l. 155.
l. 624, *clergie*. This word is used both in the sense of *clergy* and *scholars*, especially in the discussion of the ancients.

l. 627, *Troie*, gen. case.
l. 633, *homme*, sing. in form, but a collective plu. in idea.
l. 635, *consuirent*, also: *followed the ideas*.

645 Du faire *estaint(estaient)* esveillé.	They were aroused to action.
De Romme partoient à tant,	They set out from Rome thereupon,
Et s'en aloient combatant,	And went away fighting,
Et prenoient paÿs et terres	And took countries and lands
Plus par le senz que par les guerres.	More by intelligence than by wars.
650 Roys, ne tien pas sen à mençonge,	King, regard not good sense as a lie,
Ne à frivole, ne à songe.	Nor as frivolity, nor as a dream.
Sis sages à Romme estoient,	Six wise men were at Rome,
Qui du conseil s'entremetoient,	Who busied themselves with advice,
Qui toutes sciences savoient;	Who knew all sciences;
655 Pour ce, seul conseillier devoient.	For this reason, they alone were to give counsel.
Li Emperiere, duc et conte,	The Emperor, dukes, and counts,
Tout escoutoient,— c'est le conte,—	Listened to everything,— that is the tale,—
Et se*(ce)* qu'avoit d'eus esté dit	And what had been said by them
Tenu estoit sanz contredit,	Was accepted without contradiction,
660 Ou feüst à pais ou à guerre.	Whether it might be for peace or for war.
Autre tesmoing ne veil-je querre	Other witness I do not wish to seek
Que les *feiz(faiz)* aus sages de Romme,	Than the deeds of the sages of Rome,
Dont enquor parlent maint prudomme.	Of which still speak many honest men.
Des .xii. sages sunt les faiz	Of the twelve [six] wisemen the deeds are
665 En plusieurs lieus escrips et faiz.	Written and composed in several places.
Clers et chevaliers touz ensemble	Clerics and knights were all together
A Romme furent,— ce me semble,—	At Rome,— it seems to me,—
Jusque au temps du grant Challemaine,	Until the time of great Charlemagne,
Qui tant fist par senz et par paine	Who did so much by intelligence and by effort
670 Que en France clergie tourna.	That he turned clergy (scholars) to France.
Lors de Romme se destourna,	Then from Rome they [clergy] turned away,
Et quant Challemaine l'ot tost,—	And when Charlemagne had them quickly,—
De Romme clergie,— mout tost	Clergy from Rome,— very soon
Chevalerie vint en France	Knighthood came to France
675 Avec clergie, Roy, apren ce,	With clergy. King, learn this,
Et voi comment chevallerie	And see how knighthood
Touz jourz a suÿ la clergie.	Always has followed the clergy.

l. 664, *xii*. The six wisemen of l. 652 have doubled, perhaps to gain an extra syllable from *douze*.

Tout peus-tu bien par ce connestre,	Thou mayest indeed know all by this,
Que sanz clergie tu ne peus estre;	That thou canst not exist without clergy;
680 Quar se chevaliers veus avoir,	For if thou wishest to have knights,
Devant tout ce, gens de savoir Tien.	Before all that, hold people of wisdom.
Quar après les clers vendront	For, after the clerics, there will come
Chevaliers, qui te deffendront.	Knights, who will defend thee.
Et quant clergie partira,	And when clergy leaves,
685 Chevallerie après yra.	Knighthood will go afterwards.
Or es-tu bien, Roys, parcevant	Now, King, art thou indeed aware
Que la clergie va devant,	That the clergy goes ahead,
Et les chevaliers vont après?	And the knights go afterwards?
Bonne raison ci en a pres:	A good reason we have here at hand:
690 Ne va devant tout l'apotelle,	Does not the apostle go before all,
Qui en lieu de Dieu tout chatelle?	Who in place of God lodges all?
Touz sommes dessouz sa maison.	We are all beneath His house.
Veci encor autre raison:	Here is still another reason:
Celui doit au doi le feu querre	He who needs an ape in juggling
695 A cui il faut singe en jenglierre.	Must seek the fire with his own finger.
Roys, toutes eaues vont à mer;	King, all waters go to the sea;
Pour ce, doit-on clergie amer,	Wherefore, we should love clergy,
Car en clergie a-il fontaine,	For in clergy there is a fountain,
Qui ne tarist, mes clere et saine,	Which does not grow dry, but clear and wholesome,
700 Ceste fontaine si enseingne	This fountain thus teaches
Toutes ces choses, qui que s'en plaigne:	All these things, whoever may complain thereof:
Relegieus à Dieu proier,	The religious to pray to God,
Les chevaliers à guerroier;	The knights to make war;
Les Roys enseigne à gouverner,	It teaches the Kings to govern,
705 Et les juges à discerner,	And the judges to discern,
Marchans à marchander.	Merchants to do business.
Tout ce que l'en peut demander,	All that one can ask for
Peut-on en clergie trouver.	Can be found in clergy.
Ce ne peut nus homs reprouver.	No man can disapprove of that.
710 C'est droite lingne sanz oblique.	It is a straight line without curve.
Et bien apert en politique;	And well it is evident in politics;
Là treuve-l'en enseingnement,	There, is found instruction,
De touz estaz l'ordenement.	The arrangement of all positions.
Et quant clergie tel seignourie	And when clergy has such lordly dignity,
715 A, que soit de chevallerie,	As there may be from knighthood,
Le fait par le sens de nature	It does so by natural sense

l. 689, *ci en a pres*, may also read: *ci en après, hereinafter.*
l. 691, *en lieu*, also: *in a place.*
ll. 694-5 signify that the animal-trainer (intelligence) must do first what he wants his animals to be trained to do.
l. 716, *sens de nature*, also: *intelligence from nature.*

Et d'abundant par Escripture,	And abundantly by Scripture,
Dont la nature est aguisée.	By which nature is sharpened.
Ce n'est pas chose desguisée.	This is not a disguised thing.
720 Se chevallerie s'aroute	If knighthood sets out
Après de clergie la route,	After the route of clergy,
Pour savoir et pour retenir	To know and to retain
Ce que de soi ne peut tenir	What of itself it cannot hold
Parfaitement, —combien que il aient	Perfectly,— although they [the clergy] may have
725 Chevaliers poins, dont il guerroient,—	Spurred on knights, wherewith they may make war,—
Ne pourquant ne sunt mie tes,	Nevertheless they are not such
Que toutes les soutiuetés	That they may be able to know or learn
Par eus puissent savoir n'aprendre;	Through themselves all the subtleties;
En clergie les convient prendre.	In clergy it is necessary to get them.
730 Ne de guerre tout ne sara	Nor will he, who will not have in himself [something] from clergy,
Qui de clergie en soi n'ara.	Know everything about war.
Ceus qui sont clers et chevalliers	Those who are clerics and knights
Sunt par droit meillieurs batailliers.	Are by right better fighters.
Ce sont ceus qui le plus y firent,	It is they who did the most thereat,
735 Et qui plus de terres conquirent.	And who conquered more lands.
E se du tout apartenist	And if at all it were proper
Que armes clergie maintenist,	That clergy should maintain arms,
Encor pourroit-on clers trouver	Again could one find and prove
Bons chevalliers et esprouver.	Clerics as good knights.
740 Et pour ce, Roy, qui te soit fait,	And because of this, King, which may be done for thee,
Ce que je te di manifait.	What I tell thee is manifest.
Julien Cesar, qui vesquit	Julius Caesar, who lived
Grant temps et toutes terres quit	A long time, and sought and conquered all lands,
Et conquist, clerc fu-il, sanz faille.	Was a cleric(scholar), without fail.
745 Et bien feri [de] estoc et taille;	And well he thrust and cut;
Celi conquist tretout le monde,	He conquered all the world,
Si com il est, à la reonde.	Just as it is, to the cope of heaven.
D'Alexandre, d'autre partie,	Of Alexander, on the other hand,
Est-il bien droit que l'en vous die	It is indeed right that one relate *thee*
750 En ce dité aucune note,	In this "dit" some note,
Et de son mestre Aristote,	And of his teacher, Aristotle,
Par lequel Alexandre aprist	By whom Alexander learned

l. 718, *dont, with which (knowledge)*.
l. 738, *clers*, see note on l. 624.
l. 744, *cler*, see above.
l. 745, *(de)*, seems necessary, considering the modern idiom: *frapper d'estoc et de taille*.
l. 749, *vous*, another slip to 2nd. per. plu.

Ce par quoi tout le monde prist.	That by which he took all the world.
Alexandres bon clerc estoit,	Alexander was a good cleric (scholar),
755 Et grant paine et labour mestoit	And put great pain and effort
En avoir clergie et sagesce;	To have scholarship and wisdom;
Et par celle ot force et hautesse,	And by this he had strength and high position,
Par tout le monde environ.	Through all the world round about.
De Justinien, que diron?	About Justinian, what shall we say?
760 L'en en parle de toutes pars.	People speak of him everywhere.
Ne fu-il mestre des .vii. ars?	Was he not master of the seven arts?
Clerc fu ensemble et Emperiere,	He was both cleric (scholar) and Emperor,
Et Dieu et Sainte Eglise ot chiere;	And he esteemed God and Holy Church;
Celui fu clerc d'entendement,	He was a cleric in understanding,
765 Et chevallier de hardement;	And a knight in boldness;
De sens, de conseil, souverain;	Sovereign in intelligence, in counsel;
Au bataillier le premerain.	The leader in battling.
Et si fist de l'ancien droit	And so, he made the most of the ancient law,
Le plus, que l'en list orendroit;	Which one reads now;
770 Où il nous moustre que touz princes,	Wherein he shows us that all princes,
Qui ont à gouverner provinces,	Who have provinces to govern,
Avecques eus doivent avoir	Ought to have with them
Armes et les lois de savoir.	Arms and the laws of wisdom.
Ces deus choses ensemble joint;	These two things he joins together;
775 Si fait cil mal qui les desjoint.	So, that one does evil who separates them.
Par l'*Institute* fait connoistre	By the *Institutes* he makes known
Que l'un sanz l'autre ne peut estre:	That the one cannot exist without the other:
Les clers et pour cors et pour armes,	The clerics both for studies and for arms,
Les chevaliers pour porter armes.	The knights to bear arms.
780 Ce sont braz de Sainte Eglise.	They are the arms of Holy Church,
Si com l'Escripture devise.	Just as the Scripture states.
Se l'un en estoit desraché,	If the one were detached from her,
Le cors seroit trop damaché;	The body would be too much injured;
Et pour ce, doivent estre ensemble;	And for that reason, they should be together;
785 Si fait cil mal qui les dessemble.	So, he does evil who separates them.
Bien y pert dont par ceste chose,	Well does it appear, therefore, by this thing,
Que li sage sunt tiexte et glose,	That the wise are text and glossary,
Et li pur lai sont parchemin;	And the simple laymen are parchment;
Car pas ne sevent le chemin	For they know not the way

1. 776, *Institute*. The *Institutes* of Justinian state legal principles in simple terms.

ll. 780-5. Cf. *I Corinthians* 12: 12 ff. and *Colossians* 1: 18, 24.
l. 783, damaché, for damagié.

790 De droit assens et forte aller,	To go in the right direction and strongly,
Si(se) n'en vienent aus sages parler.	If they come not to speak to the wise thereof.
Pour ce, conseul, Roys, pas n'o tel,	Wherefore, King, hear not such counsel,
Qui te dit que de ton ostel	Which tells thee that from thy lodgings
Ostes les clers, mes t'en retraiz,	Thou shouldst remove the clerics, but withdraw therefrom,
795 Et avec toy les bons astraiz.	And with thee attract the good.
Quar se clers de ton regne partent,	For if clerics depart from thy realm,
Et en autres terres s'espartent,	And go off into other lands,
Chevalerie yra après.	Knighthood will go afterwards.
Qui touz jourz [se] tenne là pres,	The physician, who may always stay there nearby,
800 Li mire doit-on honnourer	Should be respected
Pour son besoing, et demourer	For his work, and one should remain
Pres de li; quar se mestier a,	Near him; for if there is need,
Le mire le conseillera.	The physician will give counsel.
Sanz clers ne peus-tu pas avoir	Without clerics thou canst not have
805 Parfaitement sens, ne savoir;	Perfectly intelligence, nor wisdom;
Sanz ceus, ne te peuz gouverner,	Without these, thou canst not govern thyself,
Ne riens connoistre, *au(ou)* discerner	Nor know, nor discern anything.
Donques ne peuz-tu sanz clers estre.	Therefore, thou canst not be without clerics.
Roys, touz ceus te feroient pestre,	King, all those would make thee eat grass,
810 Par cui feroies autrement,—	By whom thou wouldst do otherwise,—
Cil qui te dit chose autrement.	He who tells thee something else.
De ce, Roys, peuz avoir exemple	Of this, King, thou mayest have an example
De Salomon, qui fu si emple,	From Solomon, who was so great,
Si tres riche, (riche) si poteÿs,	So very rich, so powerful,
815 Et qui de nus ne fu heÿs;	And who was hated by no one;
Si vesquit-il de mout biaus jourz,	So, he lived some very fine days,
Et empais regna-il touz jours;	And in peace he reigned always;
Quar sens et droiture et raison	For intelligence, and uprightness, and reason
Touz jourz furent de sa maison.	Always belonged to his house.
820 David, son pere, ot maint contraire,	David, his father, had many a vexation,
Ne ne les pout touz à fin traire.	Nor could he bring them all to an end.
Et Salemon, qui après vint,	And Solomon, who came afterwards,
De son pere mout li souvint	Remembered very well his father

l. 799, *(se)*. Another syllable is needed for the meter and meaning.
l. 803, *le*, refers to *on* in l. 800.
l. 809, *pestre*, equivalent to: *become a brute*.
l. 814, *(riche)*, a repetition by the scribe.

Et des guerres qu'il avoit faites;	And the wars which he had made;
825 Si penssa que fussent deffaites,	And he thought that they should be done away with,
Et de celles feüst delivré,	And he should be delivered from them,
Si que il poïst en pais vivre.	So that he might live in peace.
Et de tout ce à Dieu s'apoia,	And for all this he leaned on God,
Et Diex tantoust li envoia	And God straightway sent him
830 Un sien message qui li dist:	A messenger of His who said to him:
—Roys, Dex a tout ouÿ ton dist;	"King, God has heard all thy saying;
Requier, il ne t'escondira	Ask, He will not refuse thee
De ce que ta bouche dira.	What thy mouth will say."
Lors dist-il: —Richesse, ne force,	Then said he, "Neither riches nor people,—
835 Ne d'avoir biauté ne m'esforce,	Nor to have beauty animate me,
Mes à Dieu pri devotement,—	But I pray to God devoutly,—
Quant il m'a mis si hautement,	When He has placed me in so high place,
Quant convient que sa gent gouverne,—	When it is proper that I govern His people,—
Que sens me doint dont je discerne	That He give me intelligence with which I may discern
840 Le bien, le mal, d'entre eus, par sens;	Between them,— the good, the evil,— by intelligence;
Quar sapience en moy ne sens,	For I do not perceive wisdom in me,
Et se je l'avoie, si souffit,	And if I had it, it [would] suffice,
Ne pourroie estre desconfit.	Nor could I be discomfited.
Quant sapience en moy venrra,	When wisdom comes to me,
845 Douter point ne me convenrra;	It will not be proper for me to doubt;
Quar là où sapience vient,	For there where wisdom comes,
Touz biens vennent après,— convient.	All good things come afterwards,— that is proper."
Lors le prophete a respondu:	Then the prophet answered:
—Ne te tien pas pour fol tondu;	"Regard not thyself as a shorn fool;
850 Ta responsse, que m'as rendu,	Thy reply, which thou hast made me,
A nostre Seigneur entendu.	Our Lord has heard.
Quant requis ne li as richesse,	Since thou hast not asked riches of Him,
Honneur, ne biauté, ne proesse,	Nor honor, nor beauty, nor prowess,
Ne force sus tes anemis,	Nor strength over thine enemies,
855 Mes ton cuer as seul en ce mis:	But hast set thine heart only on this:
Que sapience *aiez(aies)* sanz plus,	That thou shouldst have wisdom, nothing more,
Roys, tu l'aras et tout au plus	King, thou shalt have it and to the very greatest amount
C'onques(Qu'onques) nus homs ne pout avoir,	That never could any man have,

ll. 830 ff. Cf. *I Kings* 3: 5-14 and *II Chronicles* 1: 7-12.
l. 840, *par sens*. The MS. also permits the reading: *presens*. In that case the English would be: . . . *discern The good, the evil, among those present*.
l. 856, *sans plus*, literally: *without more*.

26   LES AVISEMENS POUR LE ROY LOYS

Et plus richesse et plus avoir.	And more riches and more property.
860 Plus fort, plus poteïs seras;	Stronger, more powerful shalt thou be;
Tes anemis seürmonteras;	Thou shalt overcome thine enemies;
Partout aras pais sanz descort;	Everywhere thou shalt have peace without discord;
De par Dieu tout ce te raport.	In the name of God I bring thee all this."
Et ce ot-il com vesqui	And this he had so long as he lived
865 De sa loi. Ne fu après qui	By His law. There was not afterwards [any one] who
Force, valour, richesse et pris	Had so much strength, valor, riches, and worth,
Tant eüst, et sen[z] rien repris.	Nor was anything taken back.
Fu sa fin à mains desreïne:	His end was to many a proof of his right:
Fu loial, bonne et enterinne.	It was loyal, good, and sincere.
870 Roys, aussi ne quier que sagesse,	King, also seek only wisdom,
Quar je te fians que pres ce	For I promise thee that beside this
Tu aras quan que tu vourras.	Thou shalt have whatsoever thou wishest.
Roys, pensse comment tu aras	King, think how thou wilt have
Mettre à fin les guerres ton pere.	To bring to an end the wars of thy father.
875 Fai que plus ta gent ne compere	See to it that thy people no longer pay for
Les choses de mauvès conseil,	The things of evil counsel,
Dont chascun parle sus son seil;	Whereof every one speaks upon his threshold;
Dont France en a mains contraire.	Whence France has many a vexation.
Par senz tost t'en pourras retraire;	By intelligence thou wilt be able soon to withdraw therefrom;
880 Car se, sages en ta besoingne,	For, if wise in thy work,
Ne croiz, certains sui, que l'aloingne,	Thou dost not believe that it [work] may push it [counsel] aside,— I am certain,—
Tu t'en pourras bien repentir.	Thou mayest indeed repent therefor.
Roys, ne te veilles consentir	King, be not willing to be in accord
En gens que n'aras esprouvé;	With people whom thou wilt not have tested;
885 Croi les anciens esprouvé,	Believe the tested old people,
Non pas les geunes jolis cointes;	Not the young, pretty fops;

l. 867, *et sen(z) riens repris*, literally: *and without anything taken back*.
l. 868, *desreïne* for *deraisne*, action of proving or supporting one's right. It might also be for *desregne* (a noun formed on *desregner*), which would mean: *a depriving of royalty, dethronement*. This meaning does not fit the verse very well.

l. 874, *ton pere*, gen. case.
l. 879, *en*, refers to *mauvès conseil*.
l. 881, *l'aloingne*, may also be for *l'aloingnes*; the *s* omitted to gain rhyme for the eye. Another possible reading is: *S'aloingne, it* [counsel] *may be rejected*.
ll. 886-7, *cointes ... acointes*. Cf. *Du Roy Phelippe*, l. 77.

Des anciannes gens t'acointes,	Acquaint thyself with the old people,
Qui t'enseingneront droit sentier;	Who will show thee the right path;
A tes gens aies cuer entier;	Be completely frank with thy people;
890 Et si ta trempe et amesure	And so, may thy character and lack of measure
Mal ait fruit qui ne se meüre.	Have an evil fruit which may not ripen.
Se bien veus avoir, ne heür,	If thou wishest to have good things, not luck,
Croi sage conseil et meür.	Believe wise and mature advice.
Touz ceus, sire, qui te riront,	All those, sire, who will laugh for thee,
895 Et ta voulenté te diront,	And tell thee thy desire,
Il ne voudront mie ton bien;	Will not wish at all thy good;
Biau te parleront et non bien.	They will speak to thee fine [language] and not good.
Le bon ami point et arguë	The good friend stings and goads
Par poingnant parolle et aguë,	By a poignant and sharp word,—
900 Souventes foiz trouvera-l'en.	One will find oftentimes.
Roboam de Jerusalem,	Rehoboam of Jerusalem,
Qui de Salemon estoit fis,	Who was son of Solomon,
A son temps en fu desconfis,	In his time was discomfited,
Quant les foles joeunes gens crut.	When he believed the foolish young men.
905 Si l'en mesavint et descrut	So, there happened ill to him therefrom, and he lost
Des .x. parties de son regne,	Some ten parts of his kingdom,
Ne onques puis n'i tira regne;	Nor ever after did he gain rule there;
Jeunes estoit, si crut les jeunes;	He was young and believed the young;
Si en perdi plumes et pennes.	So, he lost thereby plumes and feathers.
910 Il vouloit son peuple grever	He wished to weigh down his people
Et servitutes allever;	And to establish servitude;
Et li joeune s'i consentoient,	And the young consented thereto,
Mes les anxiens li ditoient	But the old stated to him
Que ne seroit ne bel ne gent	That the court of those young people
915 La cort de celle joeune gent;	Would be neither beautiful, nor nice;
Mes il n'i furent entendu.	But they were not heard there.
Et par ce, de son arc tendu,	And therefore, with his bow stretched,
Cheï à terre Roboem.	Rehoboam fell to the ground.
Un estrange Jeroboem	A stranger, Jeroboam,
920 Puis vint, qui onques bien ne fit;	Then came, who never did good;
Ainsi tourna tout à defit.	Thus he turned all to defiance.
Pour ce, Roy, conseil, qui cler voie,	Therefore, King, take counsel, which sees clearly,
Pren, et qui de loing te pourvoie,	And which from afar provides for thee,

l. 892, heür, also: uncertainty.
ll. 901 ff. Cf. *I Kings* 12 and *II Chronicles* 10 (especially verses 8 in *Kings* and 8, 13, and 14 in *Chronicles*.
l. 906, .x. parties, the ten tribes of Israel which revolted against Rehoboam.
l. 909, perdi plumes et pennes, also: *was completely ruined*.
l. 919, Jeroboem. Cf. *I Kings* 12: 20.
l. 921, defit, also: *distrust*.

Si que ne t'en vieigne meschief.	So that there may not come mischief to thee.
925 Les membres deffendront le chief,	The members will defend the head,
Le chief doit gouverner les membres;	The head should govern the members;
De ces (ces) .ii. choses, Roy, te membres.	Remember, King, these two things.
Comparaisons sunt enuieuses	Comparisons are annoying
Et de parolles venimeuses;	And of venomous words;
930 Si ne veus pas comparaison	So, I do not wish to make comparison
De nullui faire et desraison.	Of any one and [commit] injustice.
Et des clers et des chevalliers	And of the clerics and of the knights
Sunt les plus sages emparliers	The wisest counselors are
Et clergie et chevallerie.	Members both of clergy and of knighthood.
935 Chascuns en ses poinz seignourie;	Each dominates in his moments;
Mes de touz biens le fondement	But of all good things the foundation
Treuve-l'en plus parfondement	Is found more deeply
En clers que l'en ne fait en lais.	In clerics than in laymen.
La sentence donner en *lais(lois)*	To give decision in laws
940 A chascun, mes qu'à dame envie,	Invite every one except a lady,
Qui maint bon jugement desvie.	Who turns aside many a good judgment.
Et quant clers ont senz de nature	And when clerics have intelligence by nature
Et d'abundant par Escripture,	And abundantly by Scripture,
Dont connoissent les malefices,	Whereby they recognize evil deeds,
945 Il doivent bien avoir offices	They should indeed have duties
De juger, de co[n]seil baillier,	Of judging, of giving counsel,
Auxi bien com le chevallier.	As well as the knight.
Et *ce(se)* convoitise, avarice,	And if covetousness, avarice,
Orgueil, ou aucun autre vice,	Pride, or any other vice,
950 En clergie a esté trouvé,	In clergy has been found,
Aussi a-il esté prouvé	Also it has been proved
Des lais en la chevallerie;	Of laymen in knighthood;
L'un de l'autre ja ne s'en rie.	Let the one not laugh at the other.
L'en le voit *ou(au)* réaume de France,	This is seen in the realm of France,
955 Qui porte plus droite balance,	Which bears a straighter balance,
Dont aucuns en sunt orendroit,	And whence there are some right now,
Qui ne vont pas à leur endroit,—	Who do not go to their place,—
Et clers et lais trop orgueilleus.	Both clerics and too proud laymen.
Dont les haus hommes merveilleus	Then the high-placed men are astonished,
960 En sunt, quant ce sunt et maintiennent,	When they, who do not belong in their position,

l. 925, *membres*, also: *limbs*.
l. 927, *(ces)*, a repetition of the scribe.
l. 938, *l'en ne fait, is done*, expression unnecessary in the English.
ll. 943-4. Cf. ll. 716-7.

Qui à leur estat n'apartiennent.	Are and maintain this.
Des uns et des autres assez	Of the ones and of the others a rather great number
Set-l'en, en vis et trespassez,	Is known, both alive and dead,
Qui trop ont mené grant mestrise,	Who have carried too much authority,
965 Et trop ont eu convoistise,	And have had too much covetousness,
Et sunt allé en mainte terre,—	And have gone to many a land,—
Et enquor *vons(vont)*,— tout pour aquerre,	And still go,— to acquire everything,
Pour les granz gaies gaaignier.	To gain great joys.

Aucuns qui ne vont ne ne viennent,	Some who do not go and do not come,
970 Mes aus chanz leur charrue tiennent,	But in the fields hold their plough,
Et par tout le temps de leur vie	And through all the time of their lives
Le chapiau portent de soussie,	Wear the hat of worry,
Encores voit-en maintenant,	Are still seen now,
Aucuns chevalliers maintenant,	Maintaining some knights,
975 Qui autrui causes espleidient.	Who exploit cases of others.
E(Hé)! gentil Roys Loÿs, qu'en dient	Well! noble King Louis, what say those, who have in themselves
Ceus qui en eus ont bonne avise?	Good judgment, about them?
Il dient que c'est convoitisse;	They say that it is covetousness;
C'est voir: d'avarice se ceuvrent	That is true: with avarice cover themselves
980 Malz chevalliers qui ainsinc euvrent.	Evil knights, who work in this way.
Les sages pour fols les en tiennent;	The wise regard them as fools;
Les choses qu'à eus apartiennent Facent, et s'autrement le font,	The things which belong to them Let them do, and if they act otherwise,
Ne se font pas, mes se deffont.	They do not progress, but they undo themselves.
985 Fames et enfanz ont sanz faille	They have wives and children, without fail,
Pour ce que chevance ne faille;	So that goods and chattel may not be lacking;
Pensent d'avoir et d'aquerir,	They think of having and of acquiring,
Quer nul ne veut de fam perir.	For no one wishes to perish from hunger.
En maintes guises fait-en draps.	In many ways cloths are fashioned.
990 Roy, ne sai que tu entendras,	King, I know not whether thou wilt understand,
Mes je di que chevance est bonne,	But I say that chattel is good,

l. 968, *gaaiginer*. The scribe probably omitted a verse after l. 968, since there is no rhyme for *gaaignier*.
l. 972, *soussie*, also: *marigold*.

l. 984, *se font*, literally: *make themselves*. The English does not lend itself to the poet's play on *font*.
l. 991, *bonne*, also: *window pane*.

Où l'en garde et point et bonne;	Where one keeps both money and maid;
Ai(Si) la chevance est mout honorable,	So, chattel is very honorable.
Que *celle(celi)* qui *covit(covi)* a rouable,	May he who has coveted movable goods,
995 En ce rouable *puis(puisse)* comprendre	In these goods be able to include
Plusieurs clers qui bien sevent prendre	Several clerics who certainly know how to take
L'autrui argent, leur senz prendre,	The money of others, to take their ideas,
Que pour pou deüssent aprendre.	Which for little they should have learned.
Helas! comme ja de ce vice	Alas! How bound already by this vice,
1000 Liés, qu'en apelle avarice,	Which is called avarice,
Religieus et clers et lais!	Are religious and clerics and laymen!
De touz estas moult pou en lais.	Of all ranks very few do I leave out.
Du premier jusqu'au derrenier,	From the first clear to the last,
Li plus si suient li denier,	The most so pursue the pennies,
1005 Que li uns plus que autre mains	That, some more than others, less,
Anques(Onques) ont touz glueuses mains.	Ever do they all have sticky hands.
Ne je ne sai pas bien qui plus;	Nor do I know indeed who most;
Si m'esteut taire du seürplus.	So, I must be silent about the rest.
Quer uns et autres voi chacer	For I see the ones and the others hunting
1010 Pour la chevance pourchacer;	In order to pursue goods and chattel;
Et cil qui plus a, plus convoite.	And he who has most covets most.
Ce fait deable, qui acouvoite	This does the devil do, who covets
Le monde, et le tient en sa main,	The world, and holds it in his hand,
Auxi com l'oisel vient à main	Just as the bird comes to one's hand
1015 Par un pou de fausse aparance,	By a little false appearance,
Dont aus eux vient la decevance.	The deception whereof appears to the eyes.
Noz clers, non pas touz, espoussées,	Our clerics, not all, but some,
Mes aucuns, en mainsons privées Hebergent souvent,— leurs voisines;	In private houses, wedded women Often lodge,— their neighbors;
1020 Les autres ont leurs concubines,	The others have their concubines,
Et leur aprennent de natures	And teach them about nature
Et la science de mesures,	And the science of measures,
Et en tels cas sunt ceus pëours	And in such cases these are worse
Que les autres lais pechëours;	Than the other lay sinners;
1025 Quer bonne exemple moustrer doivent,	For they should show a good example,

l. 994-5, *rouable*, generally: *scraper, poker;* here seems to mean: *objects on wheels.* A double meaning is probably intended.

l. 997, *senz*, also: *positions, paths.*

Mes eux et les autres deçoivent.	But they deceive themselves and others.
Ainsi de touz estaz s'enclinent	Thus, of all positions some bow
Aucuns à mal, et se declinent.	To evil, and draw to their end.
Si est pou où n'ait à redire;	So, there is little wherein there may not be something to criticize;
1030 Mes des .ii. mauvais le mains pire	But of the two evils the less worse
Doit-on eslire et retenir,	Should be chosen and retained by him
Qui bien se veüst en droit tenir.	Who might well wish to keep himself in righteousness.
Duc Naimes fu bon chevallier,	Duke Naimon was a good knight,
Et sus touz, sages empallier;	And above all, a wise counsellor;
1035 Turpin auxinc, comment qu'en taille,	Turpin also, however one may decide,
Fu bon clerc et preuz en bataille;	Was a good cleric and valiant in battle;
Le preuz evesque Gui d'Aucerre	The valiant bishop Guy d'Auxerre
Fu sages et ynel en guerre.	Was wise and agile in war.
Ne sunt pas donc choses contraires,	Clerics and knights are, therefore, not contrary things,
1040 Ne ne sunt de divers afaires	Nor are they of different businesses,—
Clers et chevalliers, se(si) me semble.	So it seems to me.
Bien les peut-on trouver ensemble;	They may well be found together;
Si ne doit l'un de l'autre dire	So, the one should not say about the other
Chose dont nesun en(n'en a) empire	A thing whereof no one has control;
1045 Ce seroient mauvaises rimes	It would be bad rhymes
L'un à l'autre proposer crimes;	To propose crimes to each other;
Par les sentences definées	By determined judgments
Aperront les choses finées.	Things will appear ended.
Et bien voit-on les mavestez	And well does one see the evils
1050 Sus les mors et les arrestez;	Upon the dead and the arrested;
Et s'aucuns clers y a-il pris,	And if there are some clerics caught therein,
Aussi des lais a mors ou pris,	Also there are some laymen dead or caught,
Qui mestre estoient de la court,	Who were masters of the court,
Et aus clers donnoient las(la) court;	And paid court to the clerics;
1055 Et leur mesnie estoit duite	And their household was suited
A telz clers à fortune nuite,	To such clerics with injured fortune,

l. 1026, may also mean: *They and the others are deceitful.*
l. 1038, *ynel,* for *isnel.*
l. 1044, *nesun en(n'en a) empire.* Another case where the scribe seems to have written from dictation. But if *nesun* is not a negative, and *a* is not inserted, *empire* becomes a verb and the verse means: *A thing by which some one grows worse.* That would be very unusual for *nesun*, which is normally a negative and *ne* is used with it when a verb is expressed.
l. 1050, *les mors,* also: *those overtaken; mors* is then the p. p. of *mordre, to overtake.*
l. 1052, *mors,* also: *overtaken,* p. p. of *mordre, to overtake.*

	Qui leur mestre vont ensevant	Who go imitating their master,
	Si comme a esté dit devant.	Just as has been said before.
	Itelz clers manient le bobant	Such clerics fondle luxury,
1060	Et les autres bons vont bobant.	And go deceiving the other good people.
	Hé! Roys, tes .... le vesselement	Ah! King, thy .... have made their vessels
	D'or et d'argent ont fait du tien;	Of gold and of silver from thy property;
	Si leur oste et le retien	So, take it from them and retain it
	Et ce que de mal ont fait faire;	And what evil they have caused to be done;
1065	Manoirs, chastiaus dois à toi traire.	Manors, castles, thou shouldst take to thyself.
	Les autres clers et lais méans,	The other clerics and middle-class laymen,
	Qui seront bien trouvé chéans,	Who will certainly be found here,
	Honoure-les et les escoute,	Honor them and listen to them,
	Ne ne les tire, ne ne boute.	And pull them not, nor push them.
1070	Se de tel genz méans te pais,	If thou feedest thyself with such middle-class laymen,
	Soit temps de guerre ou de pais,	Whether in time of war or of peace,
	Il ne te poura meschëoir,	There can no ill happen to thee,
	Ne d'estat ne poura chëoir.	Nor canst thou fall from thy position.
	Roys, ceus ont à voir renuncié,	King, those have renounced the truth,
1075	Qui t'ont en leur dit pronuncié	Who have pronounced to thee in their "dit"
	Que clers sunt vilain et remis;	That clerics are vile and remiss;
	De folour se sunt entremis;	With folly they have busied themselves;
	Quar science est de tel endroit,	For knowledge is of such character,
	Que onques, ne ja, n'orendroit,	That never, neither now, nor henceforth,
1080	En cuer vilain ne se metreit,	Would it place itself in vile heart,
	Mes de cuer vilain se retrait.	But from vile heart it withdraws.
	En cuer vilain ne se peut mettre.	In vile heart it cannot place itself.
	Vilain ne se seit entremettre	A vile person does not know how to busy himself
	De senz, ne ne fera nul tens.	With intelligence, nor will he do so at any time.
1085	Hé! gentils Roys, raison entens:	Ah! noble King, hear reason:
	Qui est gentil, qui gentement	He is noble who nobly

l. 1061, *vesselement*. Since there is no rhyme for this word, a verse is probably omitted. Perhaps the omission comes after *tes* (which may be the poss. adj.: *thy*, or the pro.: *such men*), for *vesselement* fits well with *D'or et d'argent* of l. 1062.

l. 1067, *chéans*, for *céans*. *Chéans* is a pres. part. and adj. meaning: *weakening; lucky.*

l. 1073, *poura chëoir*, an impersonal expression with *te* understood from the preceding verse.

l. 1086, *Qui* ..... *qui*. The first *qui* is equivalent to a demonstrative.

Se maintient et honestement;	Maintains himself and honestly;
Gentilté est en loiauté	Nobility is in keeping loyalty
Garder à touz et féauté.	And fealty to all.
1090 Je di qu'en celui est noblesse	I say that there is nobility in the one
Qui droit fait, ne autrui ne blesse;	Who does right, and does not harm others;
Et cil qui autrement s'adresse,	And he who otherwise speaks,
De noble home ne tient l'adresse.	Has not the skill of a noble man.
De quelque part soit home nez,	Wherever a man may be born,
1095 Puis qu'il est sages et senez,	When he is wise and prudent,
Combien qu'il ait pou de lignage,	However little lineage he may have,
Et soit de difformé corsage,	And though he be of deformed body,
Si est-il prisiez et doutez,	So, he is esteemed and respected,
Et en haus servises boutez.	And placed in high positions.
1100 Et se de lignage royal	And if he were of royal lineage,
Estoit, et il ne fust loial,	And were not loyal,
Et science n'eüst en lui,	And had not knowledge in him,
Nuz homs n'iroit avecques lui,	No man would go with him,
Ne par droit ne seroit clamez	Nor rightly would he be called
1105 Noble, mes seroit diffamez.	Noble, but would be of ill repute.
Donques à parler proprement,	Therefore, to speak properly,
Nuls homs ne peut estre autrement	No man can be noble otherwise,
Noble, si(se) n'a en lui science;	If he has not knowledge in him;
Quar lignage y fet pou en ce.	For lineage matters little in this.
1110 Roys, les faiz de chevallerie,	King, the deeds of knighthood,
Que l'en a fait par testerie,	Which have been done through caprice,
Les doit-on tenir à prouesse?	Should they be regarded as prowess?
Certes nenil! Et donc, que *esse* (*est-ce*)?	Certainly not! And then, what are they?
C'est folie et cas d'aventure,	They are folly and a case of chance,
1115 Qui vient à tart et petit dure;	Which comes too late and lasts little;
Car s'à dis en vient bonnement,	For if to ten it turns out well,
Il en vient à mil mallement.	It turns out badly to a thousand.
Cil qui en maladie aguë,	He who, in acute sickness,
Par sa teste boit vin, se tue;	Through his whim drinks wine, kills himself;
1120 Et s'aucuns en est bien venu,	And if that has turned out well for some one,
A cas d'aventure est tenu.	It is regarded as a case of chance.
Aussi sunt les faiz de ta gent;	So are the deeds of your people;
Seigneur n'en oste, ne sergent.	Neither lord nor man of arms takes from them.
Cil est fort, qui si s'amesure;	He is strong who thus restrains himself;

l. 1111, *testerie*. Cf. l. 86 of *Des Alliés*.
l. 1119, *teste*, here a synonym of *testerie*.

l. 1123, *en oste*, also: *makes war with them*.

1125 Quar point ne passe, ne mesure, Qui puis va avant, puis arriere,	For he advances not, nor measures, Who first goes forward, then backwards,
Selonc li point et la maniere.	According to the moment and the fashion.
Toute virtu tient le milieu; Force demeure en celi lieu, 1130 Et aus .ii. bouz sient les vices. Qui du milieu se part est nices.	Every virtue holds the middle course; Strength dwells in that place, And at the two ends sit the vices. He who moves away from the middle is foolish.
Hé! Roys, ce fu bien regardé De tes gens à Courtai, par Dé! Encor en est France escharnie; 1135 Quar ta gent fu lors trop hardie Et trop pendi de celle part; Mes force du milieu depart. Trop courageus, trop couardi,	Ah! King, this was well seen By thy people at Courtrai, by God! France is still shamed for that; For thy people were then too bold And sallied too much on that side; But strength comes from the middle. Those too courageous, those too cowardly,
Ne sunt mie fort, ne hardi; 1140 Mes qui milieu tenir s'efforce, A celle virtu qu'en dit force;	Are not at all strong, nor bold; But he who strives to hold the middle, Has that virtue which is called strength;
Si ne sunt pas ceus à reprendre, Qui bien sevent le milieu prendre;	So, those are not to be reproved, Who know well how to take the middle course;
Et en ce faire clers miex voient 1145 Que les simples lais ne feroient.	And to do this, clerics see better Than simple laymen would do.
Et par plus cler entendement, Roys, de nul home hardement Riens ne vaut le sens, n'i habite,	And by clearer understanding, King, of any man with boldness Nothing is worth the intelligence, nor comes up to it,
Mes le tient-on chose despite. 1150 De ce as example en tes viandes,	But it is regarded as a despised thing. Of this thou hast an example in thy viands,
Que telles as com tu demandes, Mes se sel n'i a mis à point,	Which thou hast such as thou asketh, But if there is no salt put thereon at the proper time,
Sades ne te sembleront point. Roys, le sel est discretion, 1155 Selonc nostre exposition; En toutes choses sel couvient. Roys, d'une chose me souvient, Que fist mon sire Saint Loÿs, Qui de touz doit bien estre ouïs. 1160 Il s'apensa que l'en li die Tout le meilleur mot de clergie;	They will not seem agreeable to thee. King, the salt is discretion, According to our explanation; In all things salt is necessary. King, I remember one thing, Which my sire Saint Louis did, Who should certainly be heard by all. He thought that he should be told All the best words of clergy;

l. 1125, *mesure*, also: *calculates*.
l. 1148, *habite*. According to Godefroy *habiter* may mean *atteindre*.

Ce fu ce que il demanda	That was what he asked
Aus clers de Paris, et manda;	And ordered of the clerics of Paris;
Et il respondirent manieré	And they, erect, replied
1165 Le meilleur mot de clergie eré	The best words of traveled clergy.
En toutes choses dont avoir	In all things, therefore, there should be
Doit mesure nez en savoir;	Measure born (even) in wisdom;
Quer par sciences mesurées	For by prudent knowledge
Ont les guerres pou de durées.	Wars have short duration.
1170 Toutes choses mesure ordeinne,	Measure arranges all things,
Et jusqu'à droite fin les maine;	And leads them up to an upright end;
Si apert bien que sapience	So, it is indeed apparent that wisdom
Doit avoir sur force audience.	Should have hearing over force.
Ce t'apert, Roy, par une histoire	This is clear to thee, King, through a history
1175 De Troie, qui est moult notoire.	Of Troy, which is very famous.
Gentil Roy, escoute et enten;	Noble King, listen and hear,
Miex que ne fist ton pere enten;	Hear better than did thy father;
Un pou tes oreilles m'otroie:	Grant me a moment thine ears:
Quant destruite fu la grant Troie,	When great Troy was destroyed,
1180 Les Gregois ensemble pensoient	The Greeks together considered
A cui donner l'enneur pourroient	To whom they could give the honor
De celle grant desconfiture.	Of that great defeat.
Qui l'ot? Ajax, pour s'estature,	Who got it? Ajax, for his stature,
Chevallier fu de grant renon;	Was a knight of great renown;
1185 Ot-il pour ce le pris? Hé, non!	Did he get the prize for that reason? Well, no!
Ulixes pour sa sapience	Ulysses for his wisdom
Emporta le pris par sentence.	Carried off the prize by judgment.
Ainsinc à ceste fin ouvrerent,	Thus they worked to this end,
Qu'à Ulixes le pris donnerent;	That they gave the prize to Ulysses;
1190 Et à touz dirent encor ce:	And to all they said this again:
Que miex vaut sen que ne fait force.	That intelligence is better than is strength.
Or voiz-tu bien, Roys, ne n'en doutes,	Now thou certainly seest, King, and dost not doubt it,
Que sens trespasse choses toutes.	That intelligence surpasses all things.
Donques, Roys, ceus, où plus seras,	Therefore, King, where thou wilt be most,
1195 De science avec toi aras.	Thou shalt have those of knowledge with thee.
Sus toutes choses aime et prise	Above all things, love and esteem
Nostre Seigneur et Sainte Eglise	Our Lord and Holy Church.
Par lui peuz-tu en pais regner,	By Him thou canst reign in peace,
Et tes choses à droit mener.	And conduct thine affairs aright.

l. 1167, *nez*, is the adv. *même(even)*, says N. de Wailly, *op. cit.*, p. 501, note 2.

l. 1198, *lui*, may mean *her*, referring to *Eglise*. Cf. l. 278.

1200 L'Emperere Justinien,	The Emperor Justinian,
De catholique cretien,	Of Christian Catholic [faith],
Si nous recite en ses escripz	So recites to us in his writings
De droit, que nous lessa escripz:	About law, which he left written for us:
Les granz païs, les granz contrées,	The big countries, the big lands,
1205 Qui par lui furent conquestées,	Which by him were conquered,
Non pas par force de nul home,	Not by force of any man,
Aussi com en sa loy le nomme,	Just as he states in his law,
Mes par le non nostre Seigneur	But by the name of our Lord
Vainquoit tout et avoit l'oneur;	He conquered all and had honor;
1210 Quar Desse, qui l'en souvenoit,	For of God, who remembered him,
Le non nommoit; lors li venoit	He named the name; then victory came to him,
Victoire, et par tout esprouvé	And everywhere he had experienced
L'avoit et vite trouvé.	And quickly found it.
Pour ce, dit-il là un notable,	Wherefore, he said there a proverb,
1215 Que c'est bien chose raisonnable	That it is indeed a reasonable thing
De celui Seigneur regeïr,	To recognize that One as Lord,
Servir, honorer, obeïr,	To serve, honor, obey Him,
Pour cui l'en a auctorité,	Because of Whom one has authority,
Pris, honour avec digneté.	Esteem, honor with dignity.
1220 Si disoit:—Pour ce que nous sommes	Thus said he: "Because we are
De par Dieu seingneur sus touz homes;	Through God lords over all men,
Vers lui nous devons, nous esteuvre,	Towards Him we should, we must
Et hobeïr de bouche et d'euvre.	Be obedient both in word and in deed."
Roys de France, qui tiens ton regne	King of France, who holdest thy reign
1225 De la puissance souvereine	From the sovereign Power,
Si com trouvons en tes croniques,	Just as we find in thy chronicles,
Tu ne doiz de Dieu estre obliques,	Thou shouldst not be turned away from God,
De cui tu tiens tes seignouries,	From Whom thou holdest thy seigniories,
Tes degnetez et tes mestries,	Thy dignities and thy powers,
1230 Et aussinques de ses menistres	And also from His ministers,
Qui bons seront, non pas sophistres.	Who will be good, not sophists.
Du bon et mauvais esperite	There is good and evil spirit
A par tout, mes pren de l'eslite.	Everywhere, but take from the elite.
Ainsinques doit-il touz jours estre,	Thus it should always be,

l. 1208, *nostre Seigneur*, gen. case.
l. 1210, *Desse*, gen. case.
l. 1216, *celui Seigneur*, also: *that Lord.*
l. 1221, *seingneur*, may also be: *Seing-neur, the Lord.*
l. 1222, *esteuvre*, probably intended as a form of *estovoir.*

1235 Que cil qui ameront le mestre	That those who will love the master
La mesme doivent(Doivent la mesme) [chose] amer,	Should love the same thing,
Si(Se) ne se veullent diffamer.	If they wish not to dishonor themselves.
Et sil(cil) qui le me contredient,	And those who contradict me,
De Sainte Eglise et Deux mesdient,	Slander Holy Church and God,
1240 Et du tout en tout deshoneurent,	And dishonor all in all,
Quant Sainte Eglise et clers n'oneurent;	When they honor not Holy Church and clerics;
Quar d'eux ont-il foi et baptesme,	For from them they have faith and baptism,
Les .vii. sacremenz et le cresme.	The seven sacraments and the holy oil.
Dex fist clers, mariage; et Roys	God made clerics, marriage; and Kings
1245 Consenti es livres des Roys;	He approved in the Books of the Kings;
Et les chevalliers en l'Eglise	And the knights in the Church
Sunt fait, non pas en autre guise.	Are made, not in another way.
Là convient que ses armes prengne,	There it is necessary that he get his arms,
Et que de l'Eglise les tiengne,	And that he hold them from the Church,
1250 Là les requiert, là l'en li baille,	There he seeks them, there they are given to him,
Et puis à la mort li rebaille	And then at death he gives them back
A l'Eglise dont les ot pris;	To the Church, whence he had taken them;
Si en a l'Eglise le pris,	So, the Church has the esteem,
Quant elle l'arme et si l'atourne,	When she arms him and thus equips him,
1255 Et puis droit à son droit retourne	And then rightly, as it is proper, renders him
Chevallier. Donques qui mesdit	Knight. Therefore, he who speaks ill
De l'Eglise et de clers en dit,	Of the Church and of clerics in "dit"
Semble oisel qui son ni conchie;	Resembles a bird which makes filthy its own nest;
Si est droit que li en meschie.	So, it is right that evil befall him therefor.
1260 Tu meïsmes, Roy debonnaire,—	Thyself, good-natured King,—
Se clers et Sainte Eglise n'aire (n'ere),	If clerics and Holy Church err not,
Par cui seroies couronné,	By which thou wouldst be crowned,
Encor s'en leu pas non e[s],—	Even if thou art not in place,—

l. 1236. This verse lacks one syllable. If *chose* is the missing word, the word order must be charged in order to have only eight syllables.
l. 1245, *Consenti*, may possibly be *consecra, consecrated*, although the last three letters of the word in the MS. more closely resemble *nti*.
l. 1251, *li*. It would seem preferable to find *les* here, since *à l'Eglise* is in the next verse.
l. 1255, *droit à son droit*, a favorite expression of the poet. Cf. *Du Roy Phelippe*, l. 7, and *Un Songe*, l. 295.
l. 1260-3. The two successive rhymes (*aire* for *ere* and *e* for *es*) represent exaggerated efforts on the part of the poet to gain rhyme for the eye.

Ne reçois-tu ta dignété,	Receivest thou not thy dignity,
1265 Ta hautesse, ta majesté,	Thy highness, thy majesty,
De Sainte Eglise? Et li *jurez* (*jures*)	From Holy Church? And thou swearest to her
Que son homme es tant com *durez* (*dures*)	That thou are her man so long as thou shalt endure,
Et li seras bon et loial;	And thou shalt be good and loyal to her;
Tel est le serement royal,	Such is the royal oath,
1270 Et jusqu'à tant que ce soit fait	And until this may be done
Enterinéement de fait,	Entirely in fact,
Ne seras-tu pour Roy tenu	Thou shalt not be regarded as King,
N'à Paris comme Roy venu.	Nor come to Paris as King,
Hé! Roys pren-te garde et avise	Well, King! take care and note
1275 Que Dex est le chief de l'Eglise,	That God is the head of the Church,
Et ses membres sunt touz féaus.	And her members are all faithful.
Se tu aus membres n'es loiaus,	If thou art not loyal to the members,
A Dieu son chief fais dehonour,	To God, her head, thou doest dishonor,
Et parjure es à ton Seignour.	And thou art a perjurer to thy Lord.
1280 Pren-te garde, Roy, derechief,	Take care, King, again,
Quels senz sunt plus pres de ton chief	What ideas are nearest to thy head,
Et par *ses(ces)* senz bien tost saras	And by these ideas very soon thou shalt know
Quels genz plus pres de toy aras.	What people thou hast nearest to thee.
Oreille, eux et nez et bouche,	Ears, eyes and nose and mouth,
1285 Ceus doivent estre de ta touche,	These should be of thy test,
Et puis dois à tes mains etendre,	And then thou shouldst stretch out to thy hands,
Et à tes piez dessouz descendre;	And go down to thy feet;
De chascun membre as-tu mestier:	Thou hast need of each member:
Face dont chascun son mestier,	Let each, therefore, do its function,
1290 Et si se tieingne en son office.	And so, let it hold itself to its duty.
Gentils Roys, que veut dire ce?	Noble King, what does this mean?
Ceus qui parleront sagement,	Those who will speak wisely,
Et escouteront doucement,	And will listen sweetly,
Et d'entendement sentiront	And will perceive with understanding
1295 Ce que les parties diront,	What the parts will say,
Et tout par droit le jugeront,	And will judge righteously,
Clerement et defineront,	Clearly, and decide everything,
Ceus dois-tu pres de toy avoir;	Those, thou shouldst have near thee;
Et *se(ce)* sunt les genz de savoir.	And they are the men of wisdom.
1300 Puis prens tes mains pour batailler,	Then, take thy hands for battling,
Et tes piez dessouz pour aler,	And thy feet for going down beneath,

l. 1285, *touche*, also: *a utensil, which served to touch foods in order to detect poisons in them.*
ll. 1290-1, *office . . . dire ce*, a very poor rhyme.
l. 1295, *parties*, also: *members.*
l. 1297, *defineront*, also: *end.*

Quer tes mains,—ce peuz-tu connestre,—	For thy hands,— this thou mayest know,—
Ne te pevent bien deffensse estre,	Certainly cannot be a defense to thee,
Ne tes piez aller droitement,	Nor thy feet go straight,
1305 Se des eux n'ont avisement.	If they do not have warning from the eyes.
Pour ce, donques, à ton bien faire,	Wherefore, then, to do what is good for thee,
Sunt les eux trop plus necessaire	The eyes are very much more necessary
Que ne sunt autres membres toutes.	Than are all the other members.
Pour ce, Roy, saches et escoutes	Wherefore, King, know and hear
1310 Que, comment qu'i[l] doie avenir,	That, whatever should happen,
Doiz-tu plus pres de toy tenir	Thou shouldst keep nearer thee
Senz et savoir que autre chose;	Intelligence and wisdom than any other thing;
Droit le dit et voir le suppose.	Uprightness says so and truth supports it.
Garde donc, Roy, ce que tu jures,	Keep then, King, what thou swearest,
1315 Ne croi pas les mauvais parjures,	Believe not the evil perjurers,
Qui te conseillent desgarder	Who counsel thee to abandon
Ce que tu doiz par foy garder.	What thou shouldst keep by faith.
Pensse qu'à la mort tu vendras	Think that at death thou shalt come
A l'Eglise et là remendras;	To the Church and there shalt thou remain;
1320 Pour ce, l'arme et fai, en ta vie,	Therefore, arm her and do, in thy life,
Tant qu'après ta mort pour toy prie.	So much that, after thy death, she may pray for thee.
A ton besoing la trouveras,	In thy need thou shalt find her,
Quant loing de tes parenz seras,	When far from thy relatives thou shalt be;
Lors te seront loiaus amis	Then will be loyal friends for thee
1325 Les biens qu'en l'Eglise aras mis.	The goods which thou shalt have placed in the Church.
Gentil Roys, je t'ose bien dire	Noble King, I dare indeed to say to thee
Que ceus du réaume et de l'empire,—	That those of the kingdom and of the empire,—
Ce sunt Roys et Emperëours,—	They are Kings and Emperors,—
Plus de honours et de biens ma-ours	More honors and greater goods
1330 Ont à Sainte Eglise donné	Have given to Holy Church
Qu'enques n'ont fait cler couronné,	Than ever have done crowned clerics,
Abbé, prelat, ne apotelle.	Abbots, prelates, or apostles.
Or est donc raison bonne et belle	Now, therefore, there is a good and fine reason

Que ce qu'en avez commencié	That what *thou* hast begun
1335 Soit aussi par vous avancié;	Should also be continued by *thee;*
Car pou vaut biau commencement,	For of little worth is a fine beginning,
Si(Se) n'i a bon definement.	If there is not a good ending.
Par droit son loier en part	Rightly shares his wages
Celui qui sert et ne parsert.	That one who serves and serves not to the end.
1340 Croy ceus qui bon conseil baudront,	Believe those who will give good advice,
Et au besoing ne te faudront,—	And in need will not fail thee,—
Ceus qui bien diront et feront;	Those who will say and do good;
De ton ostel touz jours seront	Of thy household always will be
Ceus qui en bien seront metable,	Those who will be capable of being employed in what is good,
1345 Et ferme trouvé et estable,—	And will be found firm and stable,—
Fai-les avecques toy manoir,	Make them remain with thee,
Et les retien de ton manoir.	And retain them in thy manor.
Ençois que tu faces la chose,	Before thou doest a thing,
En la fin pense et te repose.	Think on the end and repose thyself.
1350 Après toy ne fay abaier	Make not poor merchants bark
Pouvres marcheanz, ne baier.	Nor gape after thee.
Aime touz par droit de nature,	Love all by right of nature,
Sages léaus plus,— c'est droiture.	Loyal wisemen, more,— that is righteousness.
S'ainsinques te veus maintenir,	If thus thou art willing to maintain thyself,
1355 Dex t'aidera à soustenir,	God will aid in sustaining thee,
Et en vendras à bonne fin.	And thou shalt come to a good end.
Roys, mon dité ci te defin;	King, here I end my "dit" for thee;
Cil qui le fist, si est ton homme;	He who composed it is thy man;
Geffroy de Paris, l'en le nomme.	Geffroy de Paris he is named.
1360 Pour ce le fist, car il voudroit	For this reason did he write it: for he would like
Ton honnour garder et ton droit.	To guard thy honor and thy right.
Se riens y a outre mesure,	If there is anything beyond measure therein,
Ou pou sal[é],— à cui la cure	Or not very witty,— to whom is of service the care
De mesurer sert et de saler?	For measuring and making it witty?

ll. 1334-5, *avez ... vous*. The poet slips into the 2nd per. plu. again.
ll. 1358 ff. These verses have been often quoted for the identification of the poet. See the Introduction, p vi.
l. 1363, *sal[é]*. An additional syllable is needed for the meter.
l. 1364, *sert*. C. V. Langlois, in *Hist. litt. de la France*, XXXV, p. 327, suggests: *c'ert* (old fut. of *être*). He translates the line: "à qui appartiendra le soin d'y mettre de la mesure et du sel?" N. de Wailly, in *Mémoires de l'Académie des Inscriptions*, t. XVIII, 2e p., pp. 498 ff. uses: *s'ert*.
l. 1364, *De mesurer ... de saler*. Because of an incorrect interpretation of this line Paulin Paris (*Les Manuscrits français de la Bibliothèque du Roi*, t. Ier, p. 327. See the Introduction, p. vi) thought that our poet was a "mesureur de sel."

1365 Je n'en quier à nul autre aler
    Mes qu'à toy, qui dois estre adres-
    se,
1367 Qui touz les mesarrans adresse.

    Explicit.

I do not seek to go to any other
Except to thee, who shouldst be the destination,
Which corrects all who have gone astray.
It is ended.

l. 1366, *addresse*, also: *skill*. Here de Wailly (*op. cit.*) suggests: "qui dois être la *règle* qui redresse tous ceux qui se trompent."

DE LA COMETE ET DE L'ECLIPSE, ET DE LA LUNE ET DU SOULAIL

Chascun me demande nouvelles,
Et j'en sai, mes *se(ce)* sunt de celles
Dont *ou(au)* monde court la matire.
Si vous en peut-on assez dire;
5 Ne pas, pour tant, chascun constre
En peut de soi sanz avoir mestre.

N'es[t]-ce pas bien nouvellete
De ce qui en France a esté?
De soulail eclipse et de lune,—
10 L'en le set,— c'est chose commune;
Et puis apparut la comete,
Assise entre double planete.
Ce fu entre Mars et Saturne,
En jenvier en ce temps noturne.
15 Puis, apres,— c'est la verité,—
Avez veü mortalité,
Chierté en sel, en vins, en blé.
La terre empres a tremblé;
La terre trembla sanz doutance:
20 N'es[t]-ce pas bien nouvel en France?

De lune eclipse apres ce vint,
A noient sa clarté devint;
Inde devint, noire et vermeille.
Dont assez de gent se merveille.
25 En la nuit d'octobre premiere
Fu la nuit en telle maniere.

Cuidez-vous que ce d'aventure
Soit avenu, ou de nature?
Je di qui veut aller à voir:
30 Et d'un et d'autre y peut avoir.
Et par ces choses nous desclere
Diex queque chose, aucun mistere,
Qui ja *ou(au)* siecle est avenu

Sus grant et sus peuple menu,
35 Et qui encores avendra,
Ne trop lonc temps remendra.

Every one is asking me for news,
And I know some, but it is of that kind,
The substance of which is current in the world.
So, one can tell you enough thereon;
Not, however, can every one know
About it of himself without having a teacher.

Is it not indeed a little news,—
What has happened in France?
An eclipse of sun and moon,—
One knows,— is a common thing;
And then appeared the comet,
Placed between a pair of planets.
It was between Mars and Saturn,
In January in that nocturnal season.
Then, afterwards,— this is the truth,—
You have seen death,
High prices in salt, in wines, in wheat.
The earth afterwards trembled;
The earth trembled without any doubt:
Is it not indeed novel in France?

An eclipse of the moon came after this,
Its brightness became drowned out;
Violet it became, black and vermilion,
At which not a few people are astounded.
On the night of October first
Was the night in such guise.

Do you think that this by chance
Happened, or naturally?
I say to him who wishes to get to the truth:
There may be therein both possibilities.
And by these things God makes known
To us something, some mystery,
Which already has happened in the world
To great and common people,
And which will happen again,
Nor will too long time remain.

Defaut de lune et de souleil,	The absence of moon and sun,
Que chascun pot vëoir *ou(à)* l'eil,	Which every one could see with his eyes
MCCC et XIIII en nombre,	In the year 1314,
40 Que sol et lune firent l'ombre,	When the sun and moon were obscured in shadow,
Pot bien estre naturement.	Could well be naturally.
Ne pas, pour tant, certainement	Not, however, certainly
Ce fu aparte demoutrée	Was this clearly demonstrated
De ce qui avint celle année:	By what happened that year:
45 Soleil et lune lors troublerent,	Sun and moon then became dim,
Quar Pape et Roy lors trespasserent.	For Pope and King then died.
Le Pape est souleil et le Roys	The Pope is the sun, and the King
Lune est, si comme verrois.	Is the moon, just as thou mightest see.
Ne cuidez pas qu'à desraison	Think not that unreasonably
50 Face telle comparaison.	I make such a comparison.
Soleil et lune sanz doutance	Sun and moon without doubt
Ont plus effect et plus puissance	Have more effect and more power
Que touz les cours celestiaux;	Than all the celestial bodies;
Auxi sus Crestiens féaux	So, upon loyal Christians
55 Pape et Roy le plus seignourient,	Pope and King hold most sway,
Le monde gouvernent et guient.	They govern and guide the world.
Ce sont les deux plus granz lumieres,	They are the two greatest lights,
Qui de touz jourz ça en arrieres	Which always previously
Et encor l'Eglise enluminent.	And still enlighten the Church.
60 Et quant leur temps vient que definent,	And when their time comes that they should die,
Le plus biau de sa clarté part.	The most beautiful of her brightness leaves.
L'Eglise bien encore y pert,	The Church loses still more thereby,
Se ces .ii. lumieres ne luisent:	If these two lights do not shine:
A Sainte Eglise mainz griez nuisent.	Many grievances injure Holy Church.
65 Mes quant cler emsemble reluient,	But when they gleam together brightly,
Les anemis si se defuient.	The enemies flee.
Tant com il luiront bien ensemble,	So long as they shine well together,
L'Eglise n'a paour que tremble.	The Church has no fear lest she tremble.
Sol et lune sunt granz seigneurs,	Sun and moon are great lords,
70 Pape et Roy les plus granz seigneurs,	Pope and King are the greatest lords,
Qui *plussance(puissance) ou(au)* monde aient haute.	Who have high power in the world.

l. 40. *firent l'ombre*, literally *formed the shadow*.

l. 46. The Pope Clement V and the King Philip IV both died in 1314.

Nequedant, touz .ii. orent saute	However, both leaped
De vie et de clarté momdaine.	From life and from worldly brightness.
Cel en est diverse semaine:	It is a different week for them:
75 Le Pape en avril,—bien m'en membre,—	The Pope in April, —well do I remember,—
Et le Roy apres en novembre:	And the King afterwards in November:
Le soleil premier, quer le Pape	The sun first, for the Pope
Premier lessa sa rouge chape;	First left his red cope;
Le Roy apres, ce fu la lune;	The King afterwards, he was the moon:
80 Et toutevoies l'ennée est une.	And, however, the year is the same.
L'eclipse *se(ce)* senefia.	The eclipse signified this.
Encor di qu'autre chose y a	Again I say that there is something else
Par cel eclipse demoustrée,	Demonstrated by that eclipse,
Qui en cel an fu desclarée.	Which in that year was made known.
85 De toute humaine créature	Of every human creature
Fist Dame Dex nostre nature;	Lord God made our nature;
Et en .ii. sexes l'ordena,	And in two sexes arranged it,
Quant à home fame amena;	When to man He led woman;
Et de touz sexes c'est la somme;	And that is the sum of all sexes;
90 Plus noble est cil de fame et home.	Most noble is that of woman and man.
Com soleil et lune ensement	As sun and moon likewise
Ou(Au) ciel ont seignouriement,	In the sky have lordship,
Si a homme et fame en ce monde,	So have man and woman in this world,
Si comme il se porte à la ronde.	Just as they go round about.
95 Mes lors de leur clarté perdirent	But then they lost some of their brightness
Et de leur non, quant se mesfirent,—	And of their name, when they did wrong,—
Homme et fame contre le Roy,—	Man and woman against the King,—
Et France mirent en desroy	And put France in confusion
Par le grant peché d'avoutire.	By the great sin of adultery.
100 Onques n'oÿ parler de pire,	Never did I hear of worse,
Nonques n'oÿ plus granz diffames,	Never did I hear greater dishonors,
Com de decevoir .ii. telz dames.	As from deceiving two such ladies.
Ne France ne fu tant triblée,	Nor was France so tormented
Comme elle fu celle journée;	As she was that day;
105 Et mout en nerci la noblesce	And much was the nobility blackened thereby

l. 94, *porte,* is singular in form just as *a* in l. 93, but the implied subject is *home et fame.*
l. 99. Three daughters-in-law of Philip IV were involved in a scandal in 1314. Two, the wives of Louis X and of Charles IV, were convicted of adultery and imprisoned; the third, Jeanne, the wife of Philip V, was exonerated. See *Du Roy Phelippe,* ll. 7 ff. and *Un Songe,* ll. 295 ff.

Pour ceux qui puis à grant destresse
En moururent en cors,— leur ame
Ou(au) ciel receive Nostre Dame,—
Quar engoisseuse mort souffrirent,
110 Et de bon cuer se repentirent.
Par ce grant eclipse, senz doute,
Sol et lune n'en virent goùte;
Ne du réaume tel diffame,
Fait en si haute et noble dame,
115 Ne povaient plus remirer;
Ainçois se voudrent adirer
De honte de ce regarder.
Or se veille chascun garder,

Et en loiauté droit se tieingne,
120 Que tel eclipse ne li vieingne.

Pour l'ordure de cel pechié
Fu soleil et lune chargié,
Et celle ordure donnerent,
Quant celle année se charcherent.

125 L'an mil CCC et XV vint
La comete qui puis devint
A noient. La comete moutre
Queque païs où se demoustre
La mort de Roy ou d'aucun prince,
130 Qui à gouverner a prouvince.
Sa propre nature *li(le)* note,
Si com nous tesmoingne Aristote.

En France l'avez bien veü:
A aucuns en est mal cheü
135 Qui estoient mout reluisant,
Qui levé sont à vent cuisant.

Ceste comete proprement

On account of those who then in great distress
Died in body,— may Our Lady
Receive their souls in Heaven,—
For they suffered a death of agony,
And earnestly repented.
Through that great eclipse, doubtless,
Sun and moon did not see a bit of this;
Nor such dishonor of the realm,
Done to so high and noble a lady,
Could they longer look at;
Rather they wished to get away
From the shame of seeing this.
Now let very one be willing to guard himself,

And keep himself upright in loyalty,
So that such an eclipse may not come to him.

On account of the filth of that sin
Were sun and moon encumbered,
And they gave off that filth,
When that year they sought each other.

In the year 1315 came
The comet which then disappeared.
The comet points out
Some country in which is shown
The death of the King or of some prince,
Who has a province to govern.
Its very nature denotes it,
Just as Aristotle testifies to us.

In France you have well seen it:
Evil has befallen therefrom to some
Who were very conspicuous,
Who are carried away in the destructive wind.

That comet properly showed

l. 106, *ceux*. The two lovers put to death were Norman officers attached to the service of the two princesses: Philippe and Gautier d'Aulnoy.
l. 108, *engoisseuse mort*. The two noblemen were tied to a horse and dragged naked over a newly ploughed field. Marguerite de Bourgogne, the wife of Louis X, was strangled in her prison in 1315, so that there would be no question about the legality of Louis' second marriage to Clémence de Hongrie.
l. 114, *noble dame*, Jeanne, Philip's wife, who was falsely accused.
l. 136, *vent cuisant*. Cf. *Un Songe*, l. 222.

La mort le Roy, nouvellement Loÿs trespassé, demoustra. 140 Cel an juing le quart jour l'ou-[vra]. Flamenz en ont grant joie eü De ce que si pou a geü:	The death of the King, Louis, recently dead. This year the fourth of June brought it about. The Flemings have had great joy From the fact that he has so little sport:
Se de vie eüst eu eloingne, A fin eüst mis leur besoingne!	If from life he had taken departure, He would have put an end to their trouble!
145 Hé! liez, loiaus, larges Loÿs, De toy sunt Flamenz esjouÿs, Mes nous en sommes doulereus. Joeune estoies et amoureus; En (n')eüssiens gardien, 150 Se tu le conseil ancien Des tiens eüsses retenu. Puis qu'ensi t'est avenu, Dex te face misericorde, Et en France pais et concorde.	Ah! Joyous, loyal, generous Louis, About thee the Flemings are overjoyed, But we are sorrowful. Young thou wast and loving; We should have a guardian, If thou the old advice Of thy people hadst remembered. Since thus it has happened to thee, May God grant thee mercy, And peace and harmony in France.
155 Entre Marz et Saturne estoit La comete, et entrepretoit Pour la cause de Marz la guerre, Dont encore n'est pais en terre,	Between Mars and Saturn was The comet, and it explained, Because of Mars, the war, From which there is not yet peace on earth,
Si comme l'en voit orendroit, 160 Mes pource que de l'autre endroit Devers Saturne s'enclinoit, Par cel enclin nous devinoit Une longue pluye ennuieuse; Quer Saturne est froide et moiteuse, 165 Et si demoure en son cours faire	Just as we see now, But because on the other side It turned towards Saturn, By that turn it foretold to us A long, annoying rain; For Saturn is cold and moist, And so remains in making its course

l. 138, *nouvellement*. This poem was evidently written not very long after Louis X's death in 1316. See also ll. 318 ff.
l. 140, *l'ou [vra]*. The end of this verse is blurred in the MS. As the rhyme requires *ra, ouvra* is the probable word.
l. 141, *Flamenz*. At the beginning of his reign the Flemings had profited by Louis' difficulties to take back the cities which Philip IV had taken from them. Louis marched against them, but had to give up his siege of Courtrai on account of the heavy rains. However, the war did not end until 1320.
l. 142, *geü*. Louis is supposed to have died from a fever he got from entering a cave to cool off after a game of *paume*, thus disregarding, evidently, the *conseil ancien* of l. 150. See *Un Songe*, l. 227.
l. 143, *eloingne*, is a noun, *removal*.
l. 148, *Joeune*. Louis was 27 years old.
l. 149, *n'eüssiens*. The scribe seems to have carried over the *n* from *en*.
l. 150. For *conseil*, see note on l. 142.
l. 158, *pais*. See note on l. 141.
l. 163, *longue pluye*. Continual rains inundated the country for four months in 1316, and led to a famine and much suffering for the poor.

DE LA COMÈTE ET DE L'ECLIPSE DE LA LUNE ET DU SOULAIL

Trente anz, ainz que puist à fin traire.	Thirty years, before it can draw to an end.
Pour ce, l'ennée fu pluieuse	Wherefore, the year was rainy
Et à toutes choses greveuse:	And grievous to all things:
Blez et toutes herbes pourries,	Grains and all grasses rotted,
170 Dont gent et bestes ont leurs vies.	From which men and animals have their lives.
Blé ne fu de furce France,	There was not wheat from much of France,
Quer il fu de male cueillance;	For it was from a bad crop;
Vins faillirent, mes qu'en Gascoingne	Wines were lacking, except that into Gascony
Et [en] Espeingne la besoingne	And into Spain the trouble
175 De la comete pas n'ala;	From the comet did not go;
Jusqu'à eux ne là pas n'ala.	Up to them, there, it did not go.
Mes par tout là où s'estendi	But everywhere, there where was extended
Sa vertu,— tant je vous en di,—	Its power,— so much do I tell you about it,—
Trouva-l'en faute de vitaille	People found lack of provisions
180 Et pou de granz et *fiens(feins)* pour paille,	And not much grain and hay for straw,
Ne seil faire ne à nous retraire	Nor did the contrary rain permit us
Ne lessa la pluye contraire;	To make or bring in rye;
Et pour ce, corrumpues furent	And for this reason, were spoiled
Les choses qui soustenir durent	The things which should sustain
185 Vie d'omme; si en mourut	Life of man; so, there died
Moult, que nuls ne les *secourus* *(secourut)*.	Many, for no one aided them.
Puis que les planettes, les signes,	Since the planets, the signs,
Le plus n'estoient pas benignes,	Mostly were not propitious,
Où la comete estoit assise,	Where the comet was located,
190 Conclurre puis en nulle guise,	I can conclude in any way,
Aussi voir com *pas(par)* decretalle,	As true as by decretal,
Qu'estre devoit l'année malle;	That the year was to be bad;
Et qui autrement le diroit,	And he who would say otherwise,
A verité contradiroit.	Would contradict truth.
195 Se nostre Roy de Saint Denise	If our King of St. Denis
Ha fait sus les mauvais jutise,	Has done justice on the evil ones,
Par bon conseil et esprouvé,	By good and tested counsel,
Des mauvestiez qu'en a trouvé	For the evils that have been found

l. 166, *Trente anz*. Saturn's "cours" is 29½ years.
l. 173, [*en*]. An additional syllable is needed for the meter.

l. 180, *fiens*, manure, does not seem correct here.
l. 181, *seil* appears to be a form of *seigle*.

En chevalliers, en clers, en lais,	In knights, in clerics, in laymen,
200 Qui demouroient en palais,—	Who were living in the palace,—
Et pour ce, venne la tempeste,—	And for this, does the tempest fan,—
N'enmy tel s'en plaint sené teste,	Not in the midst of such [a storm] does a wise head complain,
Qui encor tant pourra rater,	Who still may be able to miss fire so much,
Que sa teste en pourra grater	That he will be able to scratch his head
205 Là où pas ne li mengera;	There where it does not itch;
Mes ce sera quant Diex plaira.	But this will be when God pleases.
Qui voudra demoure à aise	Let him who will, remain at ease
De ce qui fait est, si s'en taise,	About what is done, and let him be silent thereon,
Quer le trop parler peut bien nuire,	For too much talking can indeed do injury,
210 Auxi com trop grater peut cuire.	Just as too much scratching can destroy.
En l'an apres,— bien me remembre,—	In the following years—, well do I remember,—
Ou(Au) disiesme jour de septembre	On the tenth day of September
Terre trembla par toute France.	The earth trembled throughout all France.
Plusieurs en orent merveillance,	Several were astounded thereat,
215 Mes je ne m'en merveille point:	But I am not surprised at all:
Estre pout par nature point,	It could have been not at all naturally,
Et demoustra en soi terra	And earth showed in itself
Ce qui toust en France aperra;	What soon will appear in France;
Et ja en pert une partie,	And already a part thereof appears,
220 S'il est qui bien y estudie.	If there is some one who studies well thereat.
Terremote naturement	The earthquake could have occurred naturally,
Pout estre, raisonnablement.	According to reasonable thinking.
A ce telle raison amene:	Such reasoning leads to this:
L'ennée fu de pluye plainne,	The year was full of rain,
225 Qui du ciel em-bas descendi;	Which came down from the sky;
En descendant par l'air fendi	Descending through the air it cleft
Le vent, qui terre trouva molle	The wind, which found the earth soft
Et creuse, aussi comme violle,	And hollow, just as a viol,

l. 203, *rater*, may mean *plunder*, a meaning which seems inappropriate here.
ll. 209-10. The idea of these two verses is also, in reverse order, found in *Les Avisemens*, ll. 96-7.
l, 211, *l'an apres*: 1316, the year after the comet (l. 125).

Pour les cretines qui venirent,	On account of the floods which came,
230 Et creuserent terre et fendirent,	And hollowed and cleft the earth,
Et plusieurs villes enmenerent.	And carried off several cities.
En ces creus *ses(ces)* venz se bouterent,	Into these hollows those winds pushed,
Et dedenz terre se repourent.	And were fed into the earth.
Et quant plus estre là ne pourent,	And they could no longer be there,
235 Il leur convint trouver yssue.	They had to find an exit.
Adonc fu la terre meüe(e).	Then the earth was moved.
A l'essu fu l'esmouvement	At the exit the movement of the earth
De terre en France seulement,	Was only in France,
Quer seullement fu lors en France	For only in France was there then
240 De pluye la grant habundance.	Great abundance of rain.
Et vent et pluye, qui ennuient	And wind and rain, which annoy
De legier, souvent s'entresuient;	Easily, often follow each other;
Si pout par nature, sanz bofe,	So, earth could naturally,— without jest(that is true),—
Terre trembler. Le filosofe	Tremble. The philosopher puts
245 Ceste cause que j'ai dit ores,	This cause, which I have now described,
Met *ou(au)* livre de metheores.	In the book about meteors.
Ne pas, pour tant, se senefie	Not, however, does it signify
Que terrienne seignourie	That seignorial land
S'esmouvra de sa propre ligne.	Will be moved from its own line.
250 Nous en voions ja bien le signe,	We certainly see the sign already,
Et toute apert la chose clere:	And all the matter appears clear:
France se tourne au secont frere;	France is turning to the second brother;
De fait, ce de droit estre doit.	In fact, this should be by right.
Chascun n'en lieve pas le doit;	No one raises his finger thereat;
255 Et si voit-on bien que la terre	And so, people see that the earth
S'esmeut hui et tremble par guerre,	Is agitated today and trembles through war,
Et veullent leur seingneur changer.	And they wish to change their lord.
Le Pape reveut estranger	The Pope wishes again as a stranger
La terre où fu Pape créez,	The land where he was created Pope,
260 Ne, se *sil(cil)* en est devéez,	Nor, if he is prevented from that,

l. 233, *repourent*, perfect of *repaistre*.
l. 236, *meüe(e)*. The scribe carelessly added an extra e.
l. 246, *livre de metheores*, probably a version of Aristotle's *Meteorologica*. Aristotle is also mentioned in *Les Avisemens*, 1, 751 and in *La Comète*, l. 132.
l. 252, *secont frere*, Philip V.
l. 253, *de droit*. The right of Philip, regarded as superior to the claims of Jeanne de Navarre, daughter of Louis X, is also referred to in *Du Roy Phelippe*, l. 7, and *Un Songe*, l. 294. However, this may refer to Philip's right to become regent, if this poem was written before the death of the infant King. See ll. 318 ff.
ll. 258-9. Thse lines indicate, according to N. de Wailly, *op cit.*, p. 520, that the Pope was thinking of leaving France.

De orlieus l'estude se mue.	Does his study change resting place.
Ainsi terre tremble et remue,	Thus the earth trembles and moves,
Et senefie aussi partages	And signifies also divisions
En terre, en fiez, et en hommages.	In land, in fiefs, and in homages.
265 La terre donques, qui trembla,	The earth then, which trembled,
Si com moy semble et me sembla,	Just as it seems to me and did seem to me,
Elle demoutra et denote	Showed and denotes
Mouvement de gent et note	Movement of people, and notes
Qui seront *ou(au)* réaume dispercés	Who will be scattered in the realm
270 Par les seignouries diverses.	Through the various seignories.
Ensi sera com je recorde.	Thus will it be as I relate.
Or le face Dex, senz descorde,	Now may God act, without discord,
Quer il est Souverain et Mestre	For He is Sovereign and Master
De ce qui est et qui peut estre.	Of what is and what may be.
275 En celle année, tout de pres,	In this year, quite recently,
Fu eclipse de lune epres,	There was an eclipse of the moon afterwards,
D'octobre la nuit premeraine,	The first night of October,
Que la lune estoit par tout plaine,	When the moon was entirely full,
Elle fu de couleur diverse:	It was of varied color:
280 Vert, *adurée(azurée)*, rouge, et perse.	Green, azure, red, and bluish.
Selonc ses diverses coulours	According to its various colors
Demoustre diverses doulours,	It indicates various sorrows,
Que l'Eglise a à endurer,	Which the Church has to endure
En brief temps qu'elle a à durer.	In the short time that she has to suffer.
285 Li un dessouz, l'autre desseure,	The one beneath, the other above,
En un estat ne sera heure;	In one state will not be for an hour;
Mauvestiez seront descouvertes,	Evils will be uncovered,
Et traisons toutes apartes,	And treasons all made clear,
Et gages bailliez de batailles	And gages given for battles,
290 Et sanc espandu ou entrailles.	And blood or entrails spilled.
Et apres ces adversitez	And after these adversities
Sera pais,—c'est la veritez,—	There will be peace,— that is the truth,—
Et du milieu cela vendra,	And from the middle [-class] that will come,
Qui le réaume maintendra,	Which will maintain the realm,
295 Et en son temps sera l'Eglise	And in her time the Church will be
En pais et en concorde assise,	In peace and in concord established,
Et tourneront en unité	And those will return to unity,

l. 261, *orlieus*, a form of *oreilleu, pillow*. The poet's idea is that the Pope will stay in France, thus disposing of Rome, *la terre où fu Pape créez*, l. 259.

l. 293, *milieu*. The virtue of the *milieu* is also preached in *Les Avisemens*, ll. 1131 ff.

Ceux qui sont en aversité;	Who are in hostility;
Mes ces quatre coulours passées	But these four colors will be
300 Seront, et sunt .iiii. années.	Passed away, and they represent four years
Ençois, se di-ge voirement,—	Beforehand, if I say truly,—
L'en le verra bien, se je ment.	It will certainly be seen, if I lie.
Nequedant Diex tost ou briement	However, God, soon or in brief time,
En peut faire son Jugement;	Can make His Judgment about that;
305 A son gré en peut ordener,	To His liking He can give orders,
Et à tel fin com veut mener.	And to such end as He wishes to lead to.
La lune auxi, qui se descline,	The moon also, which is waning,
De sa coulour c'est la Royne	From its color is the Queen
Climence qui refu troublée	Clemence, who again was troubled
310 Et de maint grief au cuer navrée,	And stricken in the heart with many a sorrow,
Quant son soleil le Roy perdi.	When she lost her sun, the King.
Pour ce, à m'opinion, cler di	For this reason, in my opinion, I say clearly
Que quant de son [grief] fu venue,	That when she had recovered from her grief,
Et doutoit encor d'avoir enue	And feared again to have trouble
315 Sanz laitance, la cause est celle:	Without nursling, the cause is this:
Que hoir male n'eüst, mes femelle;	That she might not have male heir, but a female;
De tant estoit plus eclipsée.	By so much was she more in eclipse.
Mes sa clarté est retournée:	But her brightness has returned:
La lune, apres Climence,— celle,	The moon, afterwards Clemence,— the latter,
320 Par la vertu d'une estancelle.	By the virtue of a spark.
Ce fu du fruit qu'elle engendra,	This was from the fruit that she engendered,
Duquel de France l'en tendra	By whom will be held the realm
Le réaume; et en ceste guise,	Of France; and in this way,
Et se(si) sera com je devise,	And so it will be, as I relate,
325 Se je n'en truis fausse ma lettre.	If I do not find my knowledge false.

l. 300, *.iiii. années.* This prediction came true in part. The war with Flanders ended four years later, in 1320.
l. 309, *Climence,* Clémence de Hongrie, second wife of Louis X.
l. 309, *refu. Cf. resont* in *Les Avisemens,* l. 19.
l. 313, [*grief*]. A monosyllabic is obviously omitted. Probably it is *grief.*
l. 318 ff. These lines seem to have been written in Nov., 1316, while the infant John I was still alive, or before his death was announced. They give a very definite date to the poem.
l. 320, *estancelle.* The spark is the infant King John I.
l. 322, *l'en.* This may refer to those who would act as regent or guardian of John,— his uncle Philip V and his mother Clémence.

Ore s'en veille entremettre	Now may God be willing to busy Himself with that
Et Dex à son gré en ordeinne,	And to His liking give orders about it,
Quer il est sus toute ouvre humaine;	For He is above all human work;
Et en face au profit commun.	And may He act for the common profit.
330 De tout ce ai-ge parllé com un,	Of all this I have spoken as one,
Et ses signes ai voulu dire,	And I have wished to describe His signs,
Que nul ne puisse contredire,	That no one may be able to contradict,
Que ne soient le plus venuz	That for the most part may not have come
Les granz signes et les menuz,	The great signs and the small ones,
335 Que Diex dist que venir devoient.	Which God said were to come.
Or n'i a, mes que se pourvoient	Now there are not any, but let all and every one
Touz et chascun pour recevoir,	Equip themselves to receive,
Selonc leurs ouvres, leur devoir,	According to their works, their task,
Quer quant li signe sont venu,	For when the signs have come,
340 Qui sont en Ecrip contenu,	Which are contained in Scripture,
Et que Diex avoit couvenant,	And which God had as a covenant,
Du Jugement le remenant	The rest of the Judgment
Vendra que l'en ne sara l'eure.	Will come when one will not know the hour.
Or serve donc Diex et honeure	Now, therefore, let every one serve and honor God
345 Chacun et de bouche et de main,	Both with mouth and with hand,
Quer nul n'i a point de demain:	For no one has therein any tomorrow:
Tout tendu tient son arc la mort;	Death holds its bow all set;
Si ne set nul où sera mort,	And no one knows where death will be,
Ne quant, ne comment. Or atende	Nor when, nor how. Now let every one be expectant
350 Et vive chascun par amende,	And live through reparation,
Quar qui ne vivra bonnement,	For whoever will not live in goodly manner
Contre lui aura Jugement.	Will have the Judgment against him.

DU ROY PHELIPPE QUI ORES REGNE

Li temps est couru et passez	The time has elapsed and gone
Que trois Roy nous sunt trespassez:	When three of our Kings died:
Phelippe, Loys, et Johan.	Philip, Louis, and John.
Or avons-nous le quart oen:	Now we have the fourth this year:
5 Phelippe, de Loys le frere,	Philip, the brother of Louis,
Qui sa raison y avoit clere,	Who for this had his title clear,
Et droit à son droit retournée,	And rightly returned to her right,
Royne, sa fame espousée,	A Queen, his wedded wife,
Qui premier estre le devoit,	Who in the first place was to be so,
10 Or l'est-elle,— chascun le voit.	Now she is,— every one sees it.
Dex les aime,— c'est veritez,—	God loves them,— that is the truth,—
Et apres,— c'est adversitez	And afterwards,— it is adversity
Qu'au commencement Deux leur moutre,—	Which at the beginning God shows them,—
Pais et honour aront tout outre,	Peace and honor they will have in addition,
15 Et si demouront souverain.	And so, they will remain sovereign.
Roys, de ton fil le premerain	King, about thy first-born son
Ne te guermente, Dex labeure;	Lament not,— God is at work;
Et se Dex plait, toust vendra l'eure,	And if it please God, soon will come the hour
Que de toy l'eir malle vendra,	When a male heir will come from thee,
20 Qui le réaume maintendra.	Who will uphold the realm.
Lesses-en Dieu, sire, entremettre,	Let God take care of that, sire,
Quar il en set plus que ma lettre;	For He knows more about it than do my letters;
Et si t'avise en ta besoingne	And so think on thy task
Que venir ne t'en peut vergoingne;	That shame cannot come to thee therefrom;
25 Ne tout ne pouras desvider,	Nor shalt thou be able to disentangle everything,
Se tu te fies en cuider.	If thou trustest to thinking.
Connois la fausseté, de voir:	Recognize hypocrisy, indeed:
Qu'en ne te puisse decevoir.	Let no one be able to deceive thee.

l. 3, Philip IV, d. Nov., 1314; Louis X, d. June, 1316; John I, infant who lived several days in Nov., 1316.
l. 4, *oen*, the year starting Nov., 1316.
l. 6, *sa raison*. Philip V (1316-22) became king after the death of his nephew, John I, who was born five months after the death of his father, Louis X. Philip had acted as regent after Louis' death. After John's death the rights of Philip over those of his niece Jeanne de Navarre, Louis' daughter, were approved at an assembly of notables in Paris, who thought that "anciens usages" prevented a woman from inheriting the throne of France, in spite of the protests of the Duke of Burgundy, Jeanne's maternal uncle.
l. 8, Royne, Philip's wife, Jeanne de Bourgogne, had been arrested after a court scandal in 1314, but was declared innocent by Parlement and restored to her position. See *La Comète*, l. 99, and *Un Songe*, ll. 295 ff.
l. 16, *fil*, Philip's son, who died Feb. 18, 1317. The poem seems to have been written shortly after that date.

Il t'esteut lessier en espasse	It is necessary for thee to give up
30 Le rivoirier et la chasse,	Fishing and hunting in a room,
Quar se au bois tu te veus ardre,	For if in the woods thou art willing to show thy eagerness,
Tu pourras bien de tes plains perdre;	Thou shalt be able to lose many of thy laments;
Garde tes levriers, tes bracheis,	Keep thy greyhounds, and thy brach hounds,
Quer petit vaut le roys d'escheis,	For little is worth the king of chess,
35 Se fierce, roc et chevaller,	If queen, rook, and knight,
Et paonnet ne peut aller.	And pawn cannot move.
Quant li roy seus et le dafin	When the king alone and the bishop
Demeurent, li geus est à fin.	Remain, the game is over.
S'esteut que li roy, senz demeure,	So, it is necessary that the king, without delay,
40 Soit mat, quant n'a qui le sequeure.	Be checkmated when he has no one to help him.
Pour ce, Roys, n'aies en despite	Wherefore, King, hold not in scorn
Tes genz, ta mesgnie petite;	Thy people, thy small household servants;
Aime chevalliers et sergens;	Love knights and men of arms;
Et si te tiens pres de tes gens.	And so, hold thyself near to thy people.
45 Se de bonne gens te tiens pres,	If thou holdest thyself near to good people,
Ja n'i vendra devant, n'apres,	Never will there come in front, nor behind,
Qui te *puis(puisse)* escheic ne mat dire,	Any one who can say "checkmated" to thee,
Ne roc, ne fierce contredire.	Nor oppose rook, nor queen.
Roc, chevallier, dafin, paon	Rook, knight, bishop, pawn
50 Ne douteras, ne q[u']un paon;	Thou shalt not fear, nor only one pawn;
Ne ja ne seront si liez	Nor will they ever be so checked
Qu'en ne les face desliez.	That one may not make them free.
L'entente de ton non parfait	Keep the meaning of thy perfect name,
Garde, si seras Roys parfait.	And thou shalt be a perfect King.
55 Ton non dit que tu doiz amer	Thy name says that thou shouldst love
Bonne gent de cuer sanz amer;	Good people of heart without bitterness;
Ton non dit que gueite es et garde.	Thy name says that thou art watchman and guard.
C'est bon non de Roy; or le garde,	It is a good name for a King; now keep it,
Si que deceü tu ne *soiez(soies)*	So that thou mayest not be deceived
60 De nul ne de nulle que oies.	By any man nor woman that thou mayest hear.

Ton non dit que tu doiz reluire	Thy name says that thou shouldst shine
Com la lampe clere et mal [*cuire*],	Like the bright lamp and destroy evil,
Conscience avoir clere et monde,	Have a conscience clear and pure,
Ouverte à Dieu et close au monde.	Open to God and closed to the world.
65 Ton non dit que tu aies bouche	Thy name says that thou shouldst have a mouth
De mains; or pensse à quoi ce touche:	Of hands; now think of what that signifies:
C'est que ta bouche ne *pramette (promette)*	It is that thy mouth should promise
Rien que ta main à fin ne mette.	Nothing which thy hand may not carry out.
Di le bien et fai qu'en le voie,	Say what is good and act that one may see it,
70 Se tu veus que Diex te pourvoie.	If thou wishest that God provide for thee.
Phelippe, dont ton propre non	Philip, thine own name, therefore,
Te moustre les pris et renon,	Shows thee the prizes and renown
Qui te doit en ton temps venir,	Which should come to thee in thy time,
Se ton non veus à droit tenir.	If thou wishest to hold rightly thy name.
75 Croy les anciens esprouvez,	Believe the tested old men,
Qui seront en ta court trouvez.	Who will be found in thy court.
Des joeunes, des jolis, des cointes,	With the young, the handsome, the fops,
Ont trop les Roys esté acointes;	The Kings have been too intimate;
Pour ce, croy le conseil meür,	Wherefore, believe mature counsel,
80 Se honneur veus avoir, n'eür.	If thou wishest to have honor, not luck.
En prendre aussinc, Roy, t'amesure,	Likewise, King, in taking, moderate thyself,
Quer en prendre convient mesure.	For moderation is proper in taking.
Pren du tien tout premierement,	Take of thine own at the very first,
Puis de l'autrui courtoisement,	Then that of others courteously,
85 Senz tondre et en cas raisonnable;	Without fleecing and in a reasonable way;
Quer c'est bien chose convenable.	For that is certainly a proper thing.
Quer ceus qui tollent et qui hapent,	For those who remove and snatch,
Trop pou voit-on que il eschapent	Too infrequently is it seen that they escape
Qu'en ne les preingne au derrenier.	Being caught at last.

l. 62, *(cuire)*. The last word of the verse is omitted from the MS. *Cuire* is suggested, because it is appropriate in meaning and for the rhyme, and is used by the author in *Les Avisemens*, l. 96 and in *La Comète*, l. 210.

l. 77, *cointes*, also mentioned in *Les Avisemens*, l. 886, in a similar rhyme with *t'acointes*.
l. 80, *n'eür*. *Seür secure*, might sound better, but the MS. has *neur*.

90 Sauver ne les peut nul denier, Ne chose qu'il aient *ou(au)* monde;	No penny can save them, Nor anything that they may have in the world;
Si com l'en voit en mer parfonde, Où touz poissons a pelle melle, Où le gros menguë le grelle, 95 Et puis sunt-il pris et mengiez; Si en sunt les petiz vengiez.	Just as one sees in the deep sea, Where there are all fishes pell-mell, Where the big one consumes the small, And then they are caught and eaten; So, the little ones are avenged.
Aussinc en ce monde qui mue Le riche le povre menguë, Et puis est-il pris et guillés, 100 Quer il se trebuche es filez; Pour ce, au luz, Roys pren ton avis;	Likewise, in this changing world The rich man consumes the poor, And then he is caught and beguiled, For he stumbles into the nets; Wherefore, King, take thy warning from the pike;
Li luz tant comme il noe vis, Des poissons prent-il sa pasture, Mes en ce met-il bien sa cure 105 De sa nature, qui se garde	The pike, so long as it swims alive, Takes its food from the fish, But in this it certainly takes care On account of its nature, which guards itself
De poisson qui a dure escharde. Sa nature le fait douter Qu'il ne s'estrangle au tranglouter	From a fish which has hard scales. Its nature makes it fear Lest it be strangled, in the swallowing,
A la parche qui a l'areste 110 Dure; li luz tout coi s'areste, Et de sa voie se destourne, Quant voit que sa queue li tourne.	On the perch, which has a hard bone; The pike, very quiet, stops, And turns from its way, When it sees that the perch turns its tail to it.
Roys Phelippe, se bien encerches, En ton royaume a mout de parches 115 Assemblées et granz et mendres, Qui n'ont pas les echardes tendres, Einçois feront mout de dangier, Se l'en les veust à tort mengier.	King Philip, if thou examinest well, In thy realm there are many perches Assembled, both great and small, Who do not have tender scales, Rather they will cause many dangers, If one should wish by mistake to eat them.
Pour ce, sire, au prendre t'avise, 120 Quar à prendre elles a maistrise, Et miex t'i vaudra sen que force.	Wherefore, sire, be on thy guard in the catching, For in catching them there is talent, And good sense will be thereat of more value to thee than strength.
Pour ce, à user de sen t'esforce,	Wherefore, strive to make use of good sense,
Et aime Dex et bonne vie,	And love God and good life,

l. 99, *guillés*, might be a mistake for *grillés*, *grilled*, but probably is *guilés*, which means *trompé, attrapé, pris par surprise*, according to Godefroy.

l. 110, *Dure*, in the MS. is the last word of l. 109, but it is really the first word of l. 110.

Et à bien faire te desvie,	And go out of thy way to do good,
125 Quar se tu cloches en droit faire,	For if thou stumblest in doing right,
Et Diex et monde aras contraire.	Thou wilt have both God and world against thee.
De ce proverbe te souvieingne:	Remember this proverb:
"Fai que doiz, et vieingne que vieigne,"	"Do what thou shouldst do, and come what may,"
Ne autre conseil ne croi pas.	And believe not other counsel.
130 Fai ta besoingne pas à pas,	Do thy task step by step,
Et point à point sanz tressaillir;	And point by point without trembling;
Si ne pourras à bien faillir,	So, thou shalt not be able to fail to do good,
Et Dex le te doint et octroie.	And may God give and grant that to thee.
134 Amen! quer *se(ce)* seroit grant joie.	Amen! For that would be great joy.
Explicit.	It is ended.

NOTE ON THE TWO LATIN POEMS OF GEFFROI

Between *Du Roy Phelippe* and *Un Songe* are found Geffroi's two Latin poems, which start on the verso of folio 50 of our manuscript and continue through folio 51. The first, *De Alliatis*, is composed of stanzas of eight decasyllabic verses with two rhymes. It urges the king, Philip V, to combat the *alliés* (1). The first stanzas are:

I

Hora, Rex, est de sompno surgere.	King, it is time to rise from sleep.
Ergo surge; cedat accidia.	Therefore, rise, let grief fall.
In te tui volunt insurgere,	Against thee thy people wish to rebel,
Ventillare vexilla regia	To wave the royal banners
In filios gentis adultere.	Against the sons of thy people, adulterously.
Nimis tua dormis milicia.	Too long thou sleepest with thy militia.
Licitum est vi vim repellere;	It is lawful to repel force with force;
Igitur, Rex, pugna pro patria.	Therefore, King, fight for thy native land.

II

Insignite, regis caractere,	Distinguished King of the French,
Rex Francorum, dormita parcius,	With the character of a king, sleep more sparingly,
Ut tu prosis et possis regere.	That thou mayest do good and be able to reign.
Populus est tibi propicius.	The people are favorable to thee.
Super femur tuum accingere,	Gird up thy thigh,
Hostes regni repellas longius.	That thou mayest farther repel the enemies of thy realm.
Tempus instat quo rupto federe	The time draws nigh when, with the alliance broken,
Patri non est subiectus filius.	The son is not subject to the father.

III

Rex, Philippe, tu regni diceris;	Philip, thou are called King of the realm;
Capud ergo subditis impera;	As Head, therefore, command thy subjects;
Tanquam clavis claudis et aperis,	Just as thou closest and openest bolts,
Claude mallis et bonis resera.	Close to the evil and open to the good.
Imitator regalis generis,	Imitator of a royal race,
Antiquorum genus regenera,	Regenerate the race of thy ancestors,
Et de flore da fructum operis,	And from a flower give the fruit of the work,

(1) Cf. Geffroi's French poem *Des Alliés*.

Tanquam a re plus Rex quam littera.	As much King in fact, rather than in name.

IV

Anixa(anxia) est nobis puerpera	Worried is the Gallic realm,
Gallicana regio gemitum,	Heaving a sigh for us,
Quia terra, ponthus et ethera	Because earth, sea, and air
Multiplicem movent excercitum.	Are putting in motion a mighty army.
Rex, extende manus ad opera,	King, extend thy hands to the tasks,
Et omnibus tuum fac debitum;	And do thy duty to all;
Quia raro timebis cetera,	For rarely wilt thou fear other things,
Si Deo cor habeas subditum.	If thou hast thy heart subject to God.

V

O Rex, et dum tue potencie	O King, and while the suburban affairs,
Suburbana consistunt subdita,	Subject to thy power, stand unshaken,
Tu predecessorum memorie	Mayest thou consider things so done
Cogita tam facta quam merita.	For the memory of thy predecessors as right.
Iam fermentum surgit malicie;	Now rises a ferment of ill-will;
Rebellantum vires debilita.	Weaken the strength of the rebels.
Alexander primus in acie,	An Alexander the First in brilliancy,
Rex, tuorum animos excita.	King, arouse the spirits of thy people.

VI

Tuis lignum accende sensibus	Kindle the firewood in thy senses;
Sis dux et lux, Rex, et lex pervia,	Be thou a leader and a light, King, and an accessible law,
Columbinus simplex in moribus,	Like a dove, simple in manners,
Sis serpentis cauptus astucia	Be thou wary with the astuteness of a serpent
Cum populi tui principibus,	With the princes of thy people,—
Inicimis potentis obvia	An astuteness that stands in the way of the enemies of thy powerful person,
Et contentus solis honoribus	And, content with honors alone,
Certantibus largire spolia.	Lavish the spoils on the fighters.

VII

Rex, dictus es Philippe lilium;	King, thou art called Philip, a lily;
Vere tu par tunc eris lilio,	Truly thou then shalt be like a lily,
Si directum tenet dominium ...	If right holds sways ...

In verses 83-8 Geffroi speaks against taxes:

Sunt spinarum pungentes stimuli,	They are the stinging goads of difficulties,

Sed tibi sit, O Rex, benignitas:	But may there be, O King, a kindness in thee:
Hanc sentiant omnes et singuli,	Let each and all feel this,
Non taillias dudum illicitas.	Not taxes a short time ago illegal.
Tui corda conserva populi.	Keep safe the hearts of your people.

The second Latin poem, *De la Création du Pape Jehan*, is written in stanzas of twelve decasyllabic verses with two rhymes, a similar arrangement to that found in *Des Alliés*. It celebrates the election of the Pope John XXII, containing observations on the etymology of the name John. As it was apparently written shortly after the election, it dates from August or September 1316, and probably is the second oldest of the eight poems. It starts with one of the already cited self-identifications of Geffroi (2):

> Natus ego G. de Parisio
> Regis huius cum adiutorio
> Cui filius est unigenitus
> Quid de papa Iohanne sentio . . .

(2) Cf. Introduction, p. vi.

UN SONGE

—Amis, ses-tu nulles nouvelles?
—Ouïl, asses. —Et quelles?
—Celles
Qui courent ou(au) monde orendroit.
—Or m'en di donc d'aucun endroit.
5 Dy-moy comment s'en va le monde.
—Il se tourne en figure ronde,
Tout environ ensi se tourne,
Et plus encor qui se bestourne,

Et qui va ce devant derriere,
10 Comme le jeu de la civiere.
Ne t'en vas-tu aparcevant
Que ce derrieres va devant?
Tost le te ferai parcevoir,
Se tu m'en vueus dire le voir.

15 Ne voiz-tu que li sougiet mestre

Huy contre raison vueullent estre,

Et par diverses regions
Ont fait leurs conspirations?
Chascun vueut estre le greigneur
20 Et contrester à son seigneur,
Mes en bref temps venrra la pluye,
Dont ce vent cherra, qui que ennuie.
Mau fait à son mestre riber
Et contre aguillon regiber.
25 —Est-ce tout? Ceci bien savoie.
—*Nenmi(Nenni)*, quer voulentiers diroie
Un songe que l'autrier songé,

Mes que j'en eüsse congé
De tel qui clerement y veïst
30 Et la verité m'en deïst.
—Or le me di. —Dire ne l'ose.

"Friend, knowest thou any news?"
"Yes, rather." "And what news?"
"That
Which is current in the world now."
"Well, then, tell me some of any kind,
Tell me how goes the world."
"It turns around in a round figure,
Everything about turns in this way,
And still more which turns upside down,
And which goes with the front behind,
As the game of the stretcher.
Art thou not perceiving
That this rear part goes in front?
Soon I shall make thee perceive it,
If thou art willing to tell me the truth thereon.
Dost thou not see that today the subjects
Wish, contrary to reason, to be masters,
And through various regions
Have formed their conspiracies?
Each one wishes to be the greater
And oppose his lord,
But in short time will come the rain,
From which that wind will fall, whoever it may annoy.
He acts badly to sport with his master
And to resist against a goad."
"Is that all? I knew that well."
"Not at all, for willingly would I tell

A dream which I dreamed the other day,
Provided that I might have permission
From such a one who might see clearly therein,
And might tell me the truth thereof."
"Now tell it to me." "I don't dare to tell it."

l. 10, *jeu de la civiere*, is also found in l. 45 of *Desputoison*. The expression generally has the idea of "the one in front, the other behind," and is used to suggest the ups and downs of life.
l. 22, *Dont*, may be the adverb *then*, but, for a discussion of wind and rain, see *La Comète*, ll. 224 ff.

—Pour quoy? —Qu'il n'i ait que- que chose Qui à touz ne doie pas plaire. Pour ce, souvent miex vaut le taire 35 Que le parler, si com l'en dit; Quer souvent peché l'en en dit. —Si fai ta protestation, Puis apres ta narration, Auxi com fait cil qui pladie, 40 Quant il doute qu'il ne mesdie. —Je ne sai pas se recevoir L'en la voudroit. —Oïl, de voir, Je m'en faiz fort. Or di sanz doute,	"Why?" "Lest there be something in it Which should not please all. For that reason, silence is often better Than speaking, just as they say; For often one says sinful things." "So, make thy protest, Then, afterwards, thy narration, Just as does the one who pleads, When he fears that he may speak ill." "I do not know if one would like To receive it." "Yes, truly, I feel confident about it. Now say on without fear,
M'oreille est preste qui t'escoute. 45 —Je le diroy dont voulentiers: Il n'a mie .v. moys entiers Que je, G., tel songe songoie En mon lit où je me dormoie: Je vi en une grant valée 50 Diverse gent entremeslée, Qui par la valée couroient, Et mout de bestes y prenoient, Et petites et granz ensemble, De maintes couleurs, ce me semble. 55 Quant couru la valée avoient, La monteigne apres chaçoient;	My ear is ready, listening to you." "I should tell it then willingly: It is not five whole months ago That I, Geffroi, dreamed such a dream In my bed where I was sleeping: I saw in a great valley Various people intermingled, Who were hunting through the valley, And caught many beasts there, Both small and large ones together, Of many colors, it seems to me. When they had run through the valley, Afterwards they hunted in the mountain;
Et quanque aloient consevant, Prenoient-il comme devant; Puis entr'eux partoient la proie, 60 Que nul autre n'en avoit joie. Le Roy la chace bien ouet, Mes au jeu des eschez jouet,	And all that they kept pursuing They caught as before; Then, among them they divided the prey, So that no other had joy therefrom. The King certainly heard the hunt, But he was playing at the game of chess,
Et tant joua,— mentir ne quier,—	And he played so much,— I don't wish to lie,—
A celui jeu de l'eschequier 65 Que pour la prise de sa gent,	At that game of the chess-board That on account of the capture of his men,

l. 47, *G*. Here the poet puts merely his initial, but in *Les Avisemens*, l. 1359 he has put his complete name.
ll. 49-79, the first episode of the dream concerns Philip IV (1285-1314).
l. 51, *couroient*, is used as a synonym of *chaçoient* in this verse.
l. 55, *couru*. See note on l. 51.
ll. 61, 62, *ouet, jouet*. This spelling of the imperfect ind. is indicated in Schwan-Behrens, *Grammaire de l'Ancien Français*, p. 239.
ll. 64 ff. It should be remembered that several chess terms have double meanings, e.g., *eschequier, royal treasure*, name given to the Parlement of various provinces; *eschec, booty*.

Que le jeu aloit damagent,	Whom the game was damaging,
Un plain eschec li fu geté,	A full check was put on him,
Dont il fu tout coy areté;	By which he was stopped very quietly;
Mes plus l'eschec li fist tel parte	But all the more did the check cause him such loss
70 Que pour prise, ne pour couverte,	That neither by capture nor covering [of chessmen]
L'eschec onques livrer ne pot.	Could he ever break the check.
Et pour ce, le Roy se repot,	And for this reason, the King was surfeited,
Comme traveilliez et lassez.	As though overworked and worn out.
A donques fu le jeu passez,	Then the game was over,
75 Et la mesgnie gresle et grosse,	And the chessmen, small and large,
Et(En) un sachet en lieu de fosse	In a bag instead of pit
Pelle melle ensemble fu mise.	Were placed pell-mell together.
Du jeu fu si com je devise;	About the game it was just as I state;
Si me parti d'ileuc à tant.	So, I departed from there at that point.
80 Puis en un pré vi esbatant	Then, in a meadow I saw disporting
Chevalliers, dames, damoisselles,	Knights, ladies, damsels,
Qui s'en trenqueroient nouvelles,	Who would drink to each other new toasts,
Et ensemble à un jeu jouaient,	And together played at a game,
Qu'au [s] Roys et aus Roynes nommoient.	Which they named the game of Kings and Queens.
85 Et celui qui sa main levoit	And the one who raised his hand
Neuviesme, Roy estre devoit.	Ninth, was to be King.
Là firent un Roy qui commande;	There they made a King who may command.
Quant commandé a, si demande,	All that he has commanded, he asks for,
Mes de tout ce que demandoit	But of all that he asked for
90 Et de ce que il commandoit,	And of what he commanded,
Faisoit-on ce que l'en vouloit.	They did what they wished.
Ensi se(ce) Roy [l'en] rigoloit;	Thus they mocked this King,
Mes mout n'ot pas son jeu tenu,	But he had not kept up his game long,
Que ne soit que fu devenu,	Lest he be [in reality] what he had become [in play],
95 Auxi voir com jour esclardi.	As truly as day dawns.
En jouant, ceci Roy perdi.	In playing, this King lost.
S'en sunt et furent esbahis	Those of the country were and had been
A merveilles ceux du paÿs.	Wonderfully astounded thereby.

l. 67. This verse may also be translated: *A full booty was thrown* or *allotted to him.*
l. 72, *repot,* perfect of *repaistre.*
l. 75, *mesgnie,* may also mean *retinue, household servants of a lord.*

l. 76, *fosse,* may also mean *grave.*
ll. 80-98. The second episode of the dream, which concerns Louis X (1314-16).
l. 92, *l'en* is needed to make eight syllables for the verse.

Et apres ceste grant merveille,	And after this great marvel,
100 D'outre cheminer n'i a pareille.	There is no equal in walking farther.
Et tant cheminé et allé	And so much did I walk and go
Qu'en une cité m'an(en) allé,	That I went off into a city,
Qui pleine estoit de grant richesse.	Which was full of great wealth.
Là une dame de noblesse	There a lady of nobility
105 Vi, qui me sembloit esbahie	I saw, who seemed to me troubled
Et durement au cuer marcie,	And harshly withered in heart,
Mes puis apres pour ma venue	But then afterwards, on account of my coming,
Un pou fu plus liée et plus drue.	She was a little more joyous and lively.
A table s'assist, ses mains leve,	She sat down at a table, raises her hands,
110 Et nous fist un gastel à feve,	And made us a cake containing a bean,
Du quel la feve trouva-elle;	Of which she found the bean;
Si en fu plus joieuse celle,	And she was more joyous because of that,
Et sa compaingnie auxi toute.	And also all her company.
Mes ceste joie fu tost route,	But this joy was soon dispelled,
115 Pource qu'elle adira sa feve.	Because she lost her bean.
Lors sembla que le cuer li creve,	Then it seemed that her heart may be breaking,
Et plus que devant fu irée,	And more than before was she distressed,
Quant sa feve vit adirée,	When she saw her bean lost,
Dont el devint trop plus petite.	On account of which, in addition, she became too much smaller.
120 D'ileuc m'en parti, franc et quitte.	From there I departed, free and tranquil.
Si trouvé puis une assemblée	And then I found an assembly
De belle gent, bien ordenée,	Of handsome people, quite prudent,
Qui avecques eux emmenoient	Who escorted with them
Un que Roy des cos apeloient.	One whom they called the King of the cocks."
125 —Et pour quoy ere ainsi nommé?	"And why was he thus named?"
—Assez brement m'ont-il nommé:	"Rather briefly they told me:
Pour ce que Dieu avoit servi,	Because he had served God,
Ot-il non de Roy deservi,	Had he merited the name of King,
Et pource que pour Dieu en terre	And because for God, on earth,

ll. 101-2. *Cheminé* and *allé* (twice) are 1st per. sing. of the perf. ind.
ll. 101-120. The third episode of the dream, which concerns John I, infant King of five days in Nov., 1316.
l. 119, *el*, this is probably the adverb meaning *otherwise, in addition,* but might be used for *elle,* to avoid an extra syllable in the verse.

l. 121, *trouvé.* This is probably the perf. like *cheminé* in l. 101, but it could be the historical pres. like *leve* in l. 109.
ll. 121-143 The fourth episode of the dream, which concerns Philip V (1316-22), who was reigning at the time the poem was written.

130	Ot labouré, pot-il aquerre	He had labored, he could gain
	Non de Roy et fait de victoire	Name of King and deed of victory
	Par une remontée histoire.	By a restaged history.
	Ceste cause m'ont-il rendu,	This reason they gave me,
	Mes pas ne l'ai bien entendu.	But I did not understand it well.
135	Et dient qu'il les gardera,	And they say that he will guard them,
	Si que grief l'en ne leur fera;	So that no one will cause them trouble;
	Ne mie ne leur sera lous,	Nor will he be a wolf to them,
	Mes com bon coc sera jalous	But like a good cock he will be jealous
	Sus la gent, et les bons oindra,	Over the people, and will anoint the good,
140	Et de ses esperons poindra	And will prick with his spurs
	Les mauvès, pour eux corrigier.	The wicked, in order to correct them.
	Apres vi plouvoir et neger,	Afterwards I saw it rain and snow,
	Mes le coc chanta, si m'esveille.	But the cock crowed, and I wake up.
	De ceci ai-ge grant merveille.	At this I am greatly astonished,
145	Et moult me resemble couvert.	And it seems to me very obscure."
	—Je le t'arai toust descouvert,	"I shall soon have disclosed it to thee,
	Et respondrai à tes demandes,	And I shall reply to thy requests,
	Puis que responsse m'en demandes.	Since thou dost ask me for a reply.
	Pour ce, te pri que tu m'escoutes:	Wherefore, I beg thee to listen to me:
150	Diex t'a moustré,— de ce n'en doutes,—	God has shown thee,— doubt it not,—
	En ceci songe, espertement,	In this dream, cleverly,
	Ce qu'est venu nouvellement.	What has recently happened.
	Tu m'as ci trois Roys recité,	Thou hast described to me here three Kings,
	Qui ont esté,— c'est verité,	Who have lived,— that is true.
155	Le quart mie nous ne leron:	The fourth we shall not leave aside:
	Au derrenier t'en parleron.	At the last we shall speak to thee about him.
	Roy d'eschez, de paume, et de feve,	Of the Kings of chess, of the game of "paume," and of the bean,
	Qui touz sunt du lignage d'Eve,	Who are all of the lineage of Eve,
	Du Roy des cos, le quart en conte,	Of the King of the cocks, the fourth in count,
160	Ne te ferai-ge pas mesconte;	I shall not make thee a miscount;
	De chascun raison te rendrai.	I shall give thee an explanation about each one.
	Le Roy d'escheis premier prendrai:	The King of chess I shall take first:
	Sil(Cil) Roy d'escheis si a esté	This one was thus [called] King of chess
	Par aucunne semblableté	By some resemblance
165	Un temps passé où l'en courut	In a past time when people hunted

ll. 161-223 give the interpretation of the first episode of the dream, that about Philip IV.

l. 165, *courut*. See note on l. 51.

Et chassa-l'en assez; or ut	And chased rather much; well this time
Se(Ce) temps son cors une grant piece;	Had its course a long period;
Lors prenoit-on chascun sa piece,	Then each one took his bit,
Lors chaçoit-on de mainte guise,	Then one hunted in many a way,
170 Et mainte grant beste y fu prise:	And many a great animal was caught there:
Juys, Templiers et Crestiens	Jews, Templars, and Christians
Furent pris et mis en liens,	Were caught and put in bonds,
Et chacié de païs en autre.	And driven from one country to another.
L'en jouet souz chapiau de fautre;	They played under hat of felt;
175 Lombars de toutes genz du monde	Usurers of all peoples of the world
Furent lors pris pour mettre en fonde;	Were then taken to put in the exchange market;
Lors par le monde pris a-l'en	Then throughout the world people made seizures
Pour aler en Jherusalem;	In order to go to Jerusalem;
Par tout prenoit-on à meësmes	Everywhere one took for himself
180 Puis cinquantiesmes, puis disiesmes.	First fiftieths, then tenths.
Chascun lors courroit et chaçoit,	Every one then ran and hunted,
Et pour son proufit pouchaçoit;	And for his profit chased;
Et le Roy qui adonc estoit	And he who was then the King
De chacier mout s'entremetoit;	Busied himself much with hunting;
185 Mes de la prise mains avoit;	But he had less of the capture.
Pour ce que du jeu mains savoit;	Because he knew less about the game;
Mes la seue gent et mesnie	But his people and retinue
Le plus prenoit toute partie;	Most often took a whole share;
Et par deça et par delà,	Both on this side and that,
190 Or vela-ci, or vela-là,	Now here, now there,
Devant, derere, et de travers,	Before, behind, and across,
Tout metoient arrere vers;	They put everything towards the rear·
De point en point, de table en table,	From point to point, from table to table,
Couroient Raatiau et Rouable,	Ran Rake and Scraper,
195 Touz aloient à la tournée;	All made the rounds;
Ensi la chace estoit menée:	Thus the hunt was conducted:
Un chascun sa part en prenoit,	Each one took his share of it,
Bien tenoit-on ce qu'en tenoit;	People held firmly what they held;
Roc, fierce, chevallier, dafin	Rook, queen, knight, bishop

l. 171. Under Philip IV persecutions were directed against the Jews and Lombards (1306, 1311); the order of the Templars was suppressed in 1312 (by the Pope Clement V at the Council of Vienne under pressure from Philip); and taxes were imposed on the properties of the Church and of religious orders.

l. 174, *jouet*. The imperf. ind.; see note on ll. 61, 62.

l. 175, *Lombars*, seems to be used in the general sense of usurers, but see note on l. 171.

200 N'i espargnoient nul afin;	Spared therein no ally;
Neïz chascun petit paonnet	Even each little pawn
Tolloit, se l'en ne li donnoit,	Took, if one did not give to him.
Ensi se(ce) temps de lors faisoit;	Thus did that epoch act;
D'où le Roy trop si s'en taisoit,	About which the King kept silent too much indeed,
205 Pource qu'il en avoit le mains,	Because he had the least of it,
Ne n'en conchioit que ses mains:	And he soiled only his hands with it:
De cent solz n'avoit que un denier,	Of one hundred sous he had only one penny,
Quer au jeu estoit derrenier.	For at the game he was last.
De ce je[u] fu ainsinc lonc temps;	That game was like that for a long time;
210 Pour ce, commença le contemps,	For that reason, began the quarrel
Si com l'en set, des alliez;	Of the allies, just as one knows.
Dont le temps fu amolliez,	Then the season became milder,
Et le chacier l'en deffendi,	And the hunting was forbidden,
Mes de la prise ne rendi	But nothing was given back of the captured booty
215 Nul riens qui faite avoit esté.	Which had been made.
En yver, non pas en esté,	In winter, not in summer,
Nous defina ce temps sauvage;	That wild season ended for us;
Si fu l'eschequier mis en cage,	And the chess-board was put in a cage,
Aussi comme en sachet de telle	Just as in a bag of cloth
220 Sanz plus traire point ne merelle;	Without any more playing;
Et de la mesgniée luysant	And some of the gleaming chess-set
A-l'en levé au vent cuisant	Was carried off in the wind destructive
Pour touz marchiez et pour suaire.	For all bargains and for a shroud.
Puis fu autre temps en chaaire,	Then another season was in charge (on the throne),
225 Qui se commença en novembre.	Which began in November.
Et se(ce) temps, si com je remembre,	And this season, just as I remember,
Roy de paume est qui de neuf part;	Belongs to the "paume" King, who starts from nine;
Ce temps se prist de celle part,	This season started from that figure,

ll. 201-2. Note that *paonnet* is made to rhyme with *donnoit*.
l. 211, *alliez*, the group which is decried in *Des Alliés*.
l. 220, *merelle*, a disk something like a checker-piece, which was used in the game of the same name; whence the expression *ne plus traire point ne merelle* means *ne plus jouer*.
l. 221, *mesgniée*, again has a double meaning, referring also to the king's retinue.
l. 222, *vent cuisant*. Cf. *La Comète*, l. 136.
l. 223. *Suaire* also may mean *pennon* or *maniple*.
ll. 224-246. These verses give the interpretation of the second episode of the dream, that about Louis X (1314-16).
l. 227, *paume*. Louis X is supposed to have died from a fever contracted after a game of "paume" (See *La Comète*, l. 142). It seems, therefore, that *paume* here refers both to the game of the dream (ll. 80-98), and to the game of "paume,,' which was very popular with royalty in the 14th and later centuries.
l. 228, *part*, literally means *place*.

	Et pour ce, est-il, selonc mon esme,	And for that reason, he is, according to my opinion,
230	Dit le Roy de paume neuviesme.	Called the King of the ninth palm.
	Ce temps, com Roy de paume, vint,	In this season he came like a "paume" King,
	Qui brement à noient devint.	Who in a short time became naught.
	Au noviesme moys prist-il regne,	In the ninth month he took reign,
	Et au noviesme lacha regne;	And in the ninth he let go his reign;
235	A prendre droit et proprement	To take rightly and properly
	Sa fin et son commencement,	His end and his beginning,
	Auxi mout joua-l'en à paume;	People also played much at "paume";
	Et pour ce, en chanta-l'en le siaume	And for this reason, they sang the psalm
	De requiem,— "De profundis."	For a requiem mass,— "De Profundis."
240	Si ne fu ce temps qu'un tandis;	So, this season was only a moment;
	Deux sait la cause et la raison,	God knows the cause and the reason,
	Mes debonnaire, en sa maison	But good-natured, in his house
	S'en dout(dort), quant venue est si jeune,	He goes to sleep, when his arrival is so recent,
	Par la parte d'une tel penne;	Through the loss of such eminence;
245	Mes autrement ne pot lors estre,	But it could not be otherwise then,
	Quer ainsi le vouloit le Mestre.	For the Master wished it thus.
	Apres ce temps autre est venu,	After this epoch another came,
	Qui fu plus brief et plus menu	Which was briefer and smaller
	Et plus passa legerement:	And passed more lightly:
250	Si ne fu ce temps que un moment.	So, this epoch was only a moment.
	Pour ce, est comparé à la feve,	For that reason, it is compared to the bean,
	Quer il vint et mourut en feve:	For it came and died as a bean:
	Y-celui temps,— si com moy semble,—	That epoch,— as it seems to me,—
	Il nasqui et mourut ensemble.	Was born and died at the same moment.
255	Hui commença, demain failli;	Today it commenced, tomorrow it ceased;
	Ainsi de vie à mort sailli,	Thus from life to death it jumped,
	Comme fait le Roy à la feve,	As does the bean King,
	Qui commence ensemble et acheve:	Who begins and ends at the same moment:
	Erinuit sera seignouriant,	Yesterday evening he will be ruling as lord,
260	Et demain povre mendiant;	And tomorrow a poor beggar;

l. 230, *paume neuviesme.* See ll. 85-6.
l. 233, *noviesme moys.* November was the ninth month of the Julian calendar.
l. 234. Louis X died June 4 (See *La Comète*, l. 140), but his posthumous heir, John I, was born and died in November. The infant's death ended the direct male line of Louis' family.

l. 239, "*De profundis,*" Psalm 129 (130, in King James version), which is said ordinarily in prayers for the dead.
ll. 247-268. These verses give the interpretation of the third episode of the dream, that about John I (1316).

De ce temps fu en tel maniere.	That epoch was like that.
Dont pité en fait mathe chiere.	Therefore, pity makes an expensive tomb for it.
Je n'en dirai plus autre chose,	I shall not say any other thing about it,
Mes tel lia qui se repose,	But it bound up one who is resting,
265 Et telle est par derrere mise	And another is placed behind
Qui par devant estoit assise.	Who was seated in front.
Plus n'en di, mes tant en sachiez:	More I do not say about it, but may you know so much:
Les jugemenz Dieu sunt cachiez.	The judgments of God are hidden.
Lors convint le grant temps venir,—	"Then it behooved the great epoch to come.—
270 Que le veille-en bien tenir!—	May people be willing to keep it well!—
Ce temps a grant victoire et force,	This epoch has great victory and strength,
Quer Jhesu Crist de tant l'esforce	For Jesus Christ fortifies it so much
Que la droite ligne a passée	That it has passed the direct line
Et,— la grace Dieu si donnée,—	And, with the grace of God so given,—
275 Que du bas de ligne paterne	That from the base of the paternal line
Montés est par la subalterne.	It has risen by the secondary [line].
Ce temps a pour Dieu labouré,	This epoch has labored for God,
Et pour ce, l'a Dieu honouré.	And for that reason, God has honored it.
En terre c'estoit entremis	On earth people undertook
280 De Dieu servir, et pour ce, mis	To serve God, and for that reason,
L'a Dieu haut, si com pert oan.	God has placed it high, just as it now appears.
Par lui fu fait Pape Joan,	By it John was made Pope,
Par lui avons de Pape don;	By it we have gift of the Pope;
Si li en fait Dieu guerredon.	So does God make to it a reward of him.
285 L'Eglise de Pape venue ere,	The Pope's Church had come [to France],
Espous li pourchaça et pere.	It procured for her a husband and father.
La foy, statuz de l'Eglise,	The faith, statutes of the Church,

l. 264, *tel*. The infant King John I.
l. 265. *telle*. The mother of John, Clémence de Hongrie, second wife of Louis X.
l. 269. Here begins the interpretation of the fourth episode of the dream,— that about the ruling King Philip V (1316-1322). The interpretation and the advice for the King's conduct continue to the end of the poem.

ll. 269-290. The words *temps* and *Roy* are more or less fused in meaning in these verses.
l. 273, *droite ligne*. The direct line of male heirs ended with the death of John. Philip V was the second son of Philip IV.
l. 282. Pope John XXII was elected in 1316 and chose Avignon for his residence.

A-il gardé en toute guise,	Has it [the King] kept in every way,
En mariage foy tenu,	In marriage he has kept faith,
290 Dont mieux li en est avenu.	Therefore, things have turned out better for him.
Son mariage en bon endroit	His marriage in good place
A gardé; et pour ce, orendroit	He has kept; and wherefore, now
Di, et ce tel [ai] raison[n]é,	I say, and I have reasoned this such,
Qu'il en est droit Roy couronné,	That he is rightly crowned King,
295 Et droit à son droit retournée	And rightly to her right returned
Royne, sa fame espousée,	Is the Queen, his wedded wife,
Qui premier estre le devoit;	Who in the first place was to be so;
Or est Royne,— l'en le voit.	Now she is Queen,— one sees that.
Ce coc est de Poitiers le Conte,	This cock is the Count of Poitiers,
300 Qui de garde en Réauté monte.	Who mounts on guard in Royalty,
Et à bonne cause et raison,	And with good cause and reason,
Coc le di par comparaison:	I call him a cock by comparison:
Coc aime sa propre geline,	A cock loves his own hen,
A lui se tient, à lui s'incline;	She relies on him, she bows to him;
305 Il la deffent et bien la garde,	He defends her and guards her well,
Voulentiers la voit et regarde.	Willingly he sees her and looks at her.
Le coc est preux, nobles et sage,	The cock is valiant, noble, and wise,
Oisel privé, non pas sauvage,	A tame bird, not wild,
Courtois, royal et couronné,—	Courteous, royal, and crowned,—
310 Tout ceci li a Diex donné,—	All this God has given to him,—
Amoureus et reconnoissant,	Loving and grateful,
Les siens poucinez repaissant,	Feeding his little chicks,
Et le grain leur donne et pourchasse	And he gives and hunts the grain for them
De leu en leu, de place en place.	From place to place, from spot to spot.
315 Tes condicions, ci nommées,	Such traits, here named,
A-l'en en ce Roy esprouvées	Have been experienced in this King
Par les faiz qui sont trespassez,	By the deeds which have occurred,
Des quiex l'en a veü assez.	Enough of which have been seen.
Et se Dex plaist, l'en en dira	And if it please God, it will be said of him
320 Qu'encores par amende yra.	That he will still improve.
Donques et puis que coc le claime,	Therefore, and since I call him a cock,
Comme bon coc, ses sougez aime,	Like a good cock, let him love his subjects,
Soit aimable et debonnaire,	Let him be amiable, and good-natured,
Et droit à chascun vueille faire,	And let him be willing to do right to every one,—

l. 288. In this verse the ideas of "temps" and "Roy" fuse completely and thereafter "Roy" is predominant.
l. 293, *ai*. An additional syllable is necessary for this verse.
ll. 295-7. These three verses are identical with ll. 7-9 of *Du Roy Phelippe*, and likewise refer to the arrest and the later exoneration of Jeanne de Bourgogne, Philip's wife.
l. 298. This verse is quite similar to l. 10 of *Du Roy Phelippe*.
l. 299. Philip V was Count of Poitiers before he became king.
l. 300. This verse may be translated: *Who mounts from guard (inferior rank) to kingship.*

325 Là où sera bien emplié;	Whereat he will be well employed;
Soit large, dous et deslié,	Let him be generous, mild, and free,
Et doint meuble, non heritage;	And let him give away goods, not inherited estates;
Quar *se(ce)* me semble estre folage	For it seems to me to be folly
De donner les païs, les terres.	To give away countries, and lands.
330 Dont l'en doit deffendre ses terres;	Therefore, one should defend his lands;
Pour ce, sunt au Roy les contrées,	For this reason, are countries, lands, and regions
Terres et regions données:	Given to the King:
Pour eus garder, pour eus deffendre	To guard and to defend those
Qui au Roy se sunt voulu rendre.	Who have wished to surrender themselves to the King.
335 Et qu'il en soit plus poteïz,	And let him be more powerful thereby,
Se de nul estoit enveïz.	If he were attacked by any one.
Trop du regne en a-l'en desjoint,	Too much has been separated from the kingdom,
Que l'en a à genz autres joint;	Which has been joined to other peoples;
Dont le réaume en est plus feible	Then the kingdom is weaker
340 Par tel don, par tel *astraleibe* (astral leibe)	By such a gift, by such an astrolabe (astral trickery)
Le Roy plus povre, et de la vient	The King is poorer, and from that it comes about
Que taillier le réaume convient;	That it is necessary to tax the kingdom;
De là viennent toustes et tailles,	Thence come pillaging and poll-taxes,
Quant le Roy chevauche en batailles;	When the King rides into battles;
345 Et quant au Temple, ne au Louvre	And when in the Temple and in the Louvre
Riens n'a, sus sa gent se recouvre;	He has nothing, from his people he provides for himself;
Quar puis que li faillent ses rentes,	For since his incomes fail him,
Sus sa gent prent et los et ventes	From his people he takes taxes on sales of land and of produce.
Pour ce, Phelippe, si te moines	For this reason, Philip, conduct thyself
350 Qu'*aiez(aies)* tez fiez et tes demoines,	That thou mayest have thy fiefs and thy domains,
Et de ton meuble soies larges;	And be generous with thy personal goods;

l. 340, *astraleibe*, an astrolabe was an instrument formerly used for obtaining the altitudes of planets and stars. The word might be here used in a figurative sense, such as *exaggerated* *measurement*. If the reading should be *astral leibe*, *leibe* might be a form of *lobe, tromperie, ruse, perfidie*.
l. 343, *toustes*. This is a form of *toltes*, which means *vol, rapine, pillage*.

S'auras escuz, lances et targes,	So, thou shalt have shields, lances and target-shields,
Et referas touz tes paÿs	And thou shalt remake all thy countries
Et tes anemis esbahis.	And thine enemies astounded.
355 En bien faire ne te doiz faindre,	In doing well thou shouldst not hesitate,
Mes, comme coc, dois oindre et poindre,—	But, like a cock, thou shouldst anoint and sting,—
Oing les bons et poing les mauvès,	Anoint the good and sting the evil,
Par droiture, touz les mauvès.	By justice, all the evil.
Et soit pastour et non pas lous	And let the King be a shepherd and not a wolf,
360 Le Roys, et, comme coc, jalous	And, like a cock, jealous
Sus sa gent et droit la maintieigne;	Over his people and upright, let him maintain them;
Si ne pourra que bien n'en vieigne.	So, it will not be possible that good not come about.
Sage soit et sa [gent] parceve,	Let him be wise and regard his people,
Si que barat ne le deceive;	So that ruse may not deceive him;
365 Ne trop ne doit pas someillier,	Nor too much should he sleep,
Mes, com coc, se doit esveillier	But, like a cock, he should be awake
Et savoir en sa court qu'en fait,	And know what is done in his court,
Souvent et miex que ceus n'ont fait,	Often and better than those have done,
Qui trop ont esté pereceux;	Who have been too lazy;
370 Pour ce, ne soit mie de ceux.	Wherefore, let him not be of those.
Mette avant et pié et oreille,	Let him put forward both foot and ear,
Et, comme bon coc, s'apareille,	And, like a good cock, let him prepare himself,
Si que lui n'a sa gent souzmise;	So that he has not his people in disdain;
Ne soit faite nulle seürmise;	Let no imposition be made;
375 France veille franche tenir.	Let him be willing to keep France free.
Or l'en doint Diex si convenir	Now may God grant to him so to agree
Qu'à nostre profit et s'onneur	That to our profit and his honor
Nous gouvernoit comme seigneur.	He govern us as lord.
De ton songe sus la matire	Upon the matter of thy dream
380 Ne te sai-ge autre chose dire.	I do not know anything else to say to thee.
Se m'exposition est voire,	If my explanation is true,
382 Une autre foiz me doit-on croire.	Another time one should believe me."

ll. 356-7, *oindre et poindre*. Cf. *Les Avisemens*, l. 144.
l. 359, *lous*. Cf. l. 137.
l. 363, *gent*, an obvious omission by the scribe.

l. 378, *gouvernoit*, a pres. subj., which is found generally in Southeastern France. See, Schwan-Behrens, *Grammaire de l'Ancien Français*, p. 234.

DES ALLIES

I

Tout auxi com par la fumée,
Qui s'en ist par la cheminée,
Le feu se moustre clerement;
Auxi de l'omme la pensée,
5 Telle com du cuer est pensée,
De fait et de bouche ensement,
Se moustre manifestement;
Il n'i faut autre esclairement;
Et auxi com de l'ente entée
10 En bonne terre fermement,
Qui se nourist moult doucement,
Auxi du bien bontés est née.

II

Ceste figure proposée,
A quel fin elle est recordée,
15 Vous raporterai-ge brement;
Je voy une gent aliée,
Mes miex diroie desliée
Plus à droit plus proprement,
Qui par son fait, apartement,
20 Moustre son mau concevement.
Autre rason n'i est trouvée
Que leur voulenté seulement.
En la fin gist l'encombrement
De la chose mal ordenée.

III

25 Tel gent dit qu'elle est engendrée
De noble sanc et alevée,
Mes il i pert mauvaisement;
Quer par leur ouvre est revelée
Leur voulenté, leur desirrée,
30 Et leur mavès proposement.
Dont il ont par deceivement
Et par mauvais enortement
D'eux mainte grant gent avuglée,
Qui en est au repentement,

I

Just as through the smoke,
Which goes out by the chimney,
The fire appears clearly;
So, the thought of man,
Such as it is thought in his heart,
In deed and in word of mouth, likewise,
Is shown clearly;
It needs no other explanation.
And just as from the grafted plant engrafted
Firmly in good earth,
Which is nourished very gently,
So, from good is kindness born.

II

This proffered figure,
For what purpose it is recorded,
I shall report to you briefly:
I see an allied people,
But rather should I say divided,
More rightly and more properly,
Which by its action, openly,
Shows its evil conception.
No other reason is found for it
Than their will only.
In the purpose lies the embarrassment
Of the affair poorly arranged.

III

Such people say that they are engendered
And issued from noble blood,
But that scarcely is apparent in them;
For by their work is revealed
Their will, their desire,
And their evil intention.
Then, they have by deception
And by their evil exhortation
Blinded many a great people,
Which is repentant,

The "alliés" (also spelled *aliés*) or "ligueurs" were largely nobles from the "petite noblesse" of the provinces, who first formed their leagues in 1314 in opposition to some of the reforms and taxes of Philip IV, and continued this opposition through the short reign of Louis X into that of Philip V. They claimed that they wanted a return to the "good old customs," but the bourgeoisie of Paris (and our poet) distrusted them, since they appeared to be attacking the crown. Geffroi's Latin poem *De Alliatis* is directed against the same group.

35 Quant voit leur fol conspirement Et leur malice desnuée.	When it sees their mad conspiracy And their malice laid bare.

IV

En une semblance fardée, Par dehors bonne et coulourée, Firent-il leur aliement, 40 Pour ce que feüst relevée Bonne coustume et ramenée. Telz estoit leur assemblement, Ce disoient premierement. Mes en leur cuer repotement 45 Leur grant malice pourpensée Estoit en leur venimement. Dont tel gent qui vilainement Ouvre, à droit vilainne est nomée.	In a painted pretence, Good on the outside and highly colored, They made their alliance, So that a good custom should be Restored and brought back. Such was their union, This they said at first. But in their hearts secretly Their great malice was meditated, In their poison. Therefore, such people, who vilely Work, rightly are called vile.

V

Elle est trop en mours disparée
50 Et de *ces(ses)* devanciers sevrée,
Qui se menerent noblement.
Il sont liguée *desliguée(deslignée)*,
 	
Conterfaite et mal alignée;
 	
En eux n'a point d'alignement.
 	
55 Leur devancier leur pensement
 	
Mirent tout en l'avencement
De nostre courone sacrée;
Et il sont au destruissement;
Ci a mauvais engendrement,
60 Mauvais fruit et male portée.
	They are too much apart in customs
	And separated from their predecessors,
	Who conducted themselves nobly.
	They are "unleagued" (degenerates)
	    leagued together,
	Counterfeit, and poorly endowed with
	    qualities;
	In them there is not any alignment of
	    good qualities.
	Their predecessors put their think-
	    ing
	Entirely on the advancement
	Of our sacred crown;
	And they are for destruction;
	There is here evil engendering,
	Bad fruit, and evil brood.

VI

Leur cause est mal enracinée, Et mal assise et pis posée; Et quant a mauvais fondement, Et que sus pierre n'est fondée, 65 Plus tost en sera afondée, Et par bien pou de ventement Tout ce cherra legierement; Quer quant un edefiement Est de terre en *baliz(balois)* bou- tée,	Their cause is poorly rooted, And poorly seated and worse placed; And since it has a poor foundation, And since it is not founded on rock, Sooner will it be overturned; And by very little blowing of the wind All this will fall lightly; For when a structure Is of earth placed in siftings,

ll. 49 ff. The agreement in this stanza is both with *gent* and with the masc. plu. idea of that word.
l. 52, *desliguée(deslignée)*, both are possible readings of the MS.
ll. 63-72. This Biblical figure (*Matt.* 7: 24-27) is also found in ll. 179 ff. of *Desputoison*.

70 Pris est tost et mellement . . .   It is taken soon and pell-mell . . .
....
   N'avoir ne peut longue durée.   Nor can it have long duration.

VII

Bien est telz gent desnaturée   Such a people is indeed perverted
Qui contre son chief est meslée,   Which is set at variance against its chief,
75 Dont el quiert son encombrement;   Whose embarrassment it seeks in addition;

Nature est en eux bestournée.   Nature is in them reversed.
Venir n'en peut bonne soudée,   A good penny's worth cannot come from them,

Puis qu'en eux la nature ment.   Since in them nature belies itself.
Guerre font sanz desfiement   They make war without challenge
80 Là où il doivent serement;   There where they owe oath of allegiance;

Foy y doit estre aussinc gardée.   Likewise should faith be kept there.
Se Ganelon nouvellement   If Ganelon again
Est venuz, mal amendement   Has come, an evil atonement
Ait-il et male destinée!   And an evil destiny may he have!

VIII

85 La personne n'est pas senée   The person is not wise
De senz qui fait à la testée,   Of sense who acts on whim,
Ne ne pense parfondement   And he does not think deeply
A quel point sera arivée,   What point he will have reached,
N'à quel fin ainsinc terminée   Nor at what goal will thus be ended
90 La chose qu'en prent asprement.   The affair which is seized violently.
Pour ce, doit faire bellement   Wherefore, he should act in handsome manner,

Que ne soit à son dampnement.   So that it may not be to his condemnation.

Penser y devroit à journée,   He ought to think thereon for a day,
Quar de mauvès commencement   For from a bad beginning
95 Estre ne peut à droitement   A good conclusion cannot be
Conclusion bonne amenée.   Rightly brought about.

IX

Quant droit li Roys ne leur devée,   When the King does not refuse them justice,

Mes raisons leur est presentée,   But satisfaction is given to them,
Leur fait font non deüement.   They perform their action improperly.
100 N'ont-il la venue et l'alée   Do they not have the right to come and go,

---

l. 70 or 71 is missing from the MS.

l. 82, *Ganelon*, the traitor of *the Chanson de Roland*, who with Naimon (*Avisemens*, l. 1033) and Turpin (*id.*,

l. 1035) is evidently regarded by our poet as historical as Charlemagne (*id.*, ll. 343, 668, 672).

l. 86, *à la testée*. For a discussion of *testerie*, see ll. 1111 ff. of *Avisemens*.

Et l'essue aussinc et l'entrée	And also the right to go out and go in,
Et au Roy et au Parlement?	Both to the King and to the Parlement?
Et les orra-l'en bonnement,	And one will hear them kindly,
Et sanz faire deportement	And without doing excess,
105 Sera leur raison escoutée.	One will listen to their claim.
Puisque ce ne font vraiment,	Since they do not do this sincerely,
Leur fait ne tien-g[e] à hardement,	I do not consider their action as boldness,
Mes à grant malice esprouvée.	But as proven great malice.

X

A tort est adonc conspirée	Wrongly, therefore, is such a region
110 Contre le Roy telle contrée;	In conspiracy against the King;
Si leur en vendra folement.	So, folly will come to them therefrom.
Trop tost,— c'est non pas *poui (pou)* hastée, —	Too soon,— that is not slightly in haste,—
Mainte teste en sera gratée,	Many a head will be removed for that,
Ainçois qu'i[l] soit au finement.	Before it is over.
115 Li Roys tout debonnairement	The King quite good-naturedly
Verra tout leur efforcement,	Will see all their striving,
Ne n'en fera autre assemblée.	And he will not make another assembly of them.
Puis yra pourveüement	Then will go with foresight
Li royal signe, ouvertement,	The royal nod, openly,
120 Qui les prendra à la volée.	Which will catch them on the fly.

XI

Souvent est tempeste donnée	Often a tempest springs
D'un vent qui vente à randonnée,	From a wind which blows impetuously,
Et puis assez par cheminement,	And then rather slowly,
Sanz faire longue demourée.	Without making a long stay.
125 Pour un pou de pluye ou rousée	For a little rain or dew
S'en vient tout à dechéement;	All comes to decay;
Et va le temps seriement	And time goes on calmly,
Et cesse le triboulement.	And the confusion (shower) ceases.
En contre la pointe aguisée	Against the sharpened point
130 Mauvais est le regibement,	Resistance is bad,
Pour ce qu'ainsi point doublement	Because thus it pricks doubly,
Et la plaie est à tart sanée.	And the wound is cured slowly (too late).

XII

Il ont fait une triboullée	They have made a March shower,
De marz, mes com blanche gellée,	But like hoar-frost,

l. 104, *deportement*, may also mean *misconduct*.
l. 128 *triboulement*, usually means *confusion*, but here there is evidently a play on words with *triboulée*, shower.

135 Tost ara fait son passement,	Soon it will have passed away;
Si leur lo. Que ne soit outrée	So will their lot be. Let not their folly
Leur folie, mes recoupée	Be overdone, but cut off
Par bon et sage ordenement.	By good and wise order.
Se ce ne font courtoisement,	If they do not do this courteously,
140 Damage y aront grandement.	They will have therein great loss.
Pour ce pri la Vierge honorée	Wherefore, I pray the honored Virgin
Qu'elle y mette hativement	That she put there hastily
Bonne pais, bon acordement,	Good peace, good accord,
Quer trop est la folie alée.	For too far has the folly gone.

XIII

145 Il sont com la beste esgarée,	They are like the strayed animal,
Qui, quant s'aperçoit adirée,	Which, when it perceives that it is lost,
Ne va pas mout seürement;	Does not go very surely;
Et se se sent avironnée	And if it feels itself surrounded
De levriers entour et serrée,	All about by hounds and hemmed in,
150 Lors li va par empirement;	Then matters become worse for it;
Ne ne peut fouïr longuement;	Nor can it flee for long,
Quer se li chien vont sagement,	For if the dogs go wisely,
Tost en sera prise cornée.	Soon will be sounded the horn for its capture.
Je ne di pas par jugement,	I do not speak by judgment,
155 Mes telz ont parlé hautement,	But such have spoken loudly,
Qui paieront ceste porée.	Who will pay for this mess.

XIV

Roys, la flour de lis esmerée	King, the pure fleur-de-lis
Blanche est comme la nof negée	Is white as the new snowfall,
Mes en la teue a dorement.	But on thine there is gilt.
160 Roys, ta flour de lis est dorée;	King, thy fleur-de-lis is guilded;
Dont charitez t'est demoutrée,	By which, charity is demonstrated to thee,
Et que vivre doiz chastement,	And that thou shouldst live chastely,
En tes .v. senz sensiblement,	In thy five senses wisely.
En ton escu de parement,	On thy shield for parade,
165 Trible à flour de lis en armée,	Triple with fleurs-de-lis in battle array,
C'est de la foy le sacrement,	That is the sacrament of faith,
Une en Déité simplement	One alone in Deity,
Et en personnes est triblée.	And in persons it is tripled.

l. 153, *prise cornée.* Cf. *Desputoison,* l. 5.
l. 161, *Dont,* may also mean: *Therefore.*
ll. 165 ff. P. Paris (See Introduction, p. viii) thinks that these lines prove that the reduction of the number of fleurs-de-lis in the King's escutcheon to three was in effect at the time of Philip the Fair (or rather Philip V). However, the first word of l. 165 could be the p.p. *triblé, riddled,* and the line could mean: "Riddled with an army of fleurs-de-lis." Likewise, *triblée* in l. 168 could be: *broken up.*

XV

Roys, telle est la fourmée fourmée
170 De l'escu qu'elle est trianglée,

Et par ceti disposement
T'est-il la Trinité notée,
Et la toue foy baptisée,
Dont tu es enoint dignement,
175 Mes li fuz senz devisement

Est un, quar singulierement
Est un Dieu. S'à toy acollée
Est telle foy hardiement.

....

180 Va, quar victoire t'est sauvée.

XVI

Et la fleur de lis est jurée
Foy, s'apres n'est à tort fausée.

Qu'es[t]-ce que grant degerement?
La flour de lis est espurée
185 Par la léauté *mesmement(esprouvée)* (contée),
Et s'est de sa gent mesmement

Du baston le conchiement,
En aront raisonnablement.
Pour ce, soit chascune avisée
190 Personne à faire amendement;
Ce(Se) ce non assez courtement,

En sera l'amende levée.

XVII

Gentilz Roys de roial lignée,
En la Royne couronnée
195 Prenez le vostre avisement,
Cez fruiz que la char naturée

Prist, qui puis fu en croiz triblée

Pour faire nostre salvement.
Ceus qui aloient humblement,

XV

King, such is the metamorphosed form
Of the shield that it is divided into three parts,

And by this arrangement
Is the Trinity denoted for thee,
And thy baptized faith,
With which thou art worthily anointed,
But the wood of the shield, without division,

Is one, for single
Is one God. If to thee is joined
Such faith boldly.

....

It goes, for victory is saved for thee.

XVI

And the fleur-de-lis is sworn
Faith, if afterwards it is not wrongly falsified.

What is this great turning aside?
The fleur-de-lis is purified
By tested loyalty,

And if likewise the filthiness of its people
Is [purified] with the cudgel,
They will have a reasonable treatment.
Wherefore, let each person be advised
To make reparation;
If this [is] not [done] in short enough time,
The reparation for it will be raised.

XVII

Noble King of royal lineage,
From the crowned Queen
Take thy judgment,
These fruits, which the flesh formed of nature
Took, which flesh was later tormented on the cross
To bring about our salvation.
Those who went humbly,

---

l. 179. This verse is omitted in the MS.
l. 185. This verse is obviously incorrect. The rhyme requires a word in *ée* and *esprouvée* is suggested. *Contée* is written in small letters at the end of the line in the MS., but it does not have enough syllables. *Racontée* is a possibility.
l. 195, *Prenez le vostre*. The poet here and elsewhere (See stanza XIX) slips into 2nd pr. plu. forms, but in the English translation the 2nd per. sing. is continued.

200 Obéissanz outréement, 　Retint à lui sanz dessevrée. 　Et par telz, sanz delaiement,	Obeying absolutely, He held to himself without separation. And through such people, without delay,
Roys, amirauz, devotement 　Vindrent à foy crestiennée.	Kings, emirs, devoutly Came to Christian faith.

XVIII

205 Nostre Sires fait sa moustrée
　　D'estelles en lune eclipsée
　　Et en souleil diversement;
　　Et li quatre vent font meslée
　　En l'air et mainte rencontrée
210 Et li quatre ausinc element.
　　L'iau a divers contenement,
　　La terre rafait mouvement,
　　Et bien faillent. Foiz est troublée,

　　La mort chevauche durement;
215 Si di, ne ne puis autrement:
　　Li mondes est en Galilée.

XIX

　　Roys, l'année est pieça passée
　　Que la chose est recitée,
　　Qui doit venir certainnement;
220 D'Ysaïe fu racontée,
　　Qui dit que montaigne en valée
　　Vendroit et en abaissement,

　　Si que l'en yroit plainement
　　Par tout sanz espéeschement.
225 Tost vous sera, Roys, exposée
　　Ceste parolle espertement,
　　Quar selont mon entendement
　　Pour vous fu dite et raportée.

XX

　　Hé, Roys, la montaigne eslevée,
230 Qui doit em-bas estre versée
　　Et venir à declinement,
　　C'est l'orgueil de la gent faée,
　　Qui contre toy *c'est(s'est)* forcenée,
　　Que mettras à terminement,
235 Et tetout à plain, vraiement;
　　Si que ta gent paisiblement
　　Vive qui d'eux estoit foulée.

XVIII

Our Lord makes his display
Of stars while the moon is in eclipse
And in sun eclipse variously;
And the four winds cause confusion
In the air, and many a conjuncture,
And the four elements likewise.
The water has varying content,
The earth readjusts movement
And they certainly decline. Faith is troubled,

Death rides harshly;
So I say, nor can I do otherwise:
The world is like a Galilee.

XIX

King, the year has long ago passed
When the matter is related,
Which is to come certainly;
By Isaiah it was recounted,
Who said that a mountain
Would come into a valley and into a depression,

So that one would go smoothly
Everywhere without obstacle.
Soon this saying will be explained
To thee, King, clearly,
For according to my understanding
For thee it was said and related.

XX

Well, King, the high mountain,
Which is to be cast down
And come to decline,
Is the pride of the bewitched people,
Who against thee have become maddened,
Which thou shalt put to an end,
And quite smoothly, truly;
So that thy people peacefully
May live, who by them were trampled.

ll. 221-4. Cf. *Isaiah* 40: 4, "Every valley shall be exalted, and every mountain and hill shall be made low; and the crooked shall be made straight, and the rough places plain."

Souffrir est desheritement :
Or en pren donques venchement,
240 Que ta parsonne en soit doutée.

XXI

Tu doiz estre pierre adurée,
E[t] glaive asceré et espée,
Pour maintenir ton tenement,
Si que ne soit pas mesprisée
245 France, en ton temps, ne diffamée,
Dont tu as le couronnement.
Des mauvais fai corrigement,
Et contre eux te tieing roidement;

Ton estat honourablement
250 Garde, et ta gent tieing franchement :
Adont regneras seürement.
252 Explicit : ma rime est finée.

To suffer that, is to be disinherited :
Now, therefore, take vengeance on them,
So that thy person may be feared of them.

XXI

Thou shouldst be a durable stone,
And a glaive of steel and a sword,
To maintain thy holdings,
So that France may not be scorned,
Nor defamed, in thy time,
France, whose crown thou hast.
Correct the evil ones,
And against them hold thyself rigidly,
Guard thy position honorably,
And hold thy people sincerely :

Then thou shalt reign in surety.
Explicit : my rhyme is ended.

LA DESPUTOISON DE L'EGLISE DE ROMME ET DE L'EGLISE DE FRANCE POUR LE SIEGE DU PAPE

I *(Romme)*

A droit me plaing, qui sui Romme nommée.
E(Hé)! pourquoi donc pas ne [me] complaindroie?
Trop esloingniée est ma grant renommée;
En Occidant d'Oriant se desvoie.
5 Outre les monz a-l'en prise cornée
De ce que tant lonc temps chacé avoie.
Mauvais levriers si la chace ont tournée
Que j'en sui vuide; autres en ont la proie.

Rightly do I complain,— I who am named Rome.
Well, why then should I not complain?
Too far away is my great renown;
From the Orient to the Occident it wanders.
Beyond the mountains they have sounded the horn for the capture
Of what I had hunted so long.
Bad hounds have so turned the hunt
That I am empty-handed; others have the prey.

II *(France)*

De quelle proie te veus, Romme, complaindre?
10 Es[t]-ce pource que le Pape est venu
Par de deça? Ne t'en doiz mie plaindre.
Ne l'as-tu pas assez delà tenu?

Lesse-le-nous par devers nous remaindre,
Pour conforter nostre peuple menu.
15 Le tien seingneur ne peus-tu pas contraindre;
Li de nostre est, quant nous est avenu.

Of what prey dost thou wish to complain, Rome?
Is it because the Pope has come
On this side? Thou shouldst not complain.
Hast thou not kept him long enough on that side?

Allow him to remain for us in our presence,
To comfort our common people.
Thy lord thou mayest not constrain;
He is ours, when he has come to us.

III *(R.)*

Ceste venue n'est pas mout raisonnable:
Pour moy lessier qui sui le chief du monde!
Ce n'est raison, ne chose convenable,
20 Que mon evesque et pere me confonde,—

This coming is not very reasonable:
To leave me, who am the head of the world!
It is not right, nor a proper thing,
That my bishop and father should confound me,—

---

l. 2, [*me*]. An extra syllable is needed for the meter.

l. 5, *prise cornée*. This expression is also found in *Des Alliés*, l. 153.

Qui me lessoit toute seulle à ma table,	Who left me all alone at my table,
Et qui de moy se chaçoit,— et reponde.	And who drove himself from me,— and that he should hide himself.
Il ne m'a pas en rien trouvé coupable,	He has not found me guilty in anything,
Mes l'ai servi et amé d'amour monde.	But I have served and loved him with pure love.

IV (F.)

25 Celle amour monde, dont tu aimes le Pape,	This pure love, with which thou lovest the Pope,
Est tout pour ce que la pecune en aies.	Is entirely for the money that thou mayest get from him.
En grant pene es et doutes que t'eschape.	Thou art in great pain, and fearest lest it escape thee.
La pecune aimes, et pour celle t'esmaies.	Thou lovest money, and for that, art thou worried.
De quel proufit t'estoit la rouge chape?	Of what profit was the red cloak to thee?
30 A ce besoing qu'ores as, bien l'essaies;	In this need which thou hast now, thou art indeed testing it;
Si peuz bien dire: prise es dessouz trape,	So, thou mayest very well say: thou art caught beneath a trap,
Quant mire n'as qui garisse tes plaies.	When thou dost not have a doctor who may cure thy wounds.

V (R.)

De plus grant plaie ne puis estre ferue,	With a greater wound I cannot be struck,
Que quant le Pape n'est pres de mon costé.	Than when the Pope is not near my side.
35 Mon solaz ai et ma joie perdue;	I have lost my solace and my joy;
Nul vaillant homme ne vien en mon oté(hosté).	No valiant man comes into my hostelry.
Rome la grant, et qu'es-tu devenue?	Rome the great, and what art thou become?
Par quel raison t'a-l'en ton pere osté?	For what reason has thy father been taken from thee?
Empereour n'i chevauche par rue,	The Emperor does not ride through the streets,
40 Ne Pape auxi ne s'i est acoté.	Nor has the Pope either been escorted there.

VI (F.)

Lesse le Pape et lesse l'Emperiere;	Leave aside the Pope and leave aside the Emperor;
Assez lonc temps chiez toy les as eü.	Long enough thou hast had them in thy country.

l. 22, *reponde*, may also have the more usual meaning, *answer back*.

Trop mal en as usé *sa(ça)* en ar-
rere*(arriere)*.
Ne te merveille, si t'en est me-
scheü;
45 Or t'a fait Diex le jeu de la
civiere;
Pour ce, chanter te convient de heü.

Apres le biau, apres la belle chiere,

Ne t'esmerveille, s'il a sus toy
pleü.

Thou hast made too bad use of them
in times past.
Be not astounded if evil has befallen
thee;
Now God has played for thee the game
of the stretcher;
Wherefore, it behooves thee to sing
noisily.

After the fine weather, after the fine
cheer,

Be not surprised if it has rained up-
on thee.

VII *(R.)*

Bien me souffrisse d'avoir une tel
pluie,
50 Qui ne m'est douce, mes à perte
me tourne.
C'est une pluye qui de pieça m'en-
nuie;
Quer bien richesse et pris de moi
destourne.
Ce n'est pas droit que le mari de-
fuie
La seue fame, ne qu'autre part se-
journe.
55 Et il le fet. Riens n'est qui tant
me nuie;
Pour ce, li pri que vers moi se re-
tourne.

Well might I suffer from having such
a rain,
Which is not gentle to me, but turns to
a loss for me.
It is a rain which has annoyed me for
a long time;
For it certainly turns wealth and in-
fluence from me.
It is not right that the husband flee
from
His wife, nor that he sojourn elsewhere.

And he does that. There is nothing
which injures me so much;
Wherefore, I beg him to return to me.

VIII *(F.)*

D[u] retourner ne fai mie parolle.

Tes chardonnaus ne nous donnas-
tu, Romme?
Par devers nous postulas apostole;

60 Tes genz y vindrent et senz con-
trainte d'ome.

About his returning I do not say a
word.
Didst thou not give us thy cardinals,
Rome?
In our presence thou didst nominate an
apostle (Pope);
Thy people came there and without
constraint from any one.

---

l. 45, *le jeu de la civiere*, see l. 10 of *Un Songe*.
l. 46, *heü*, is probably *hu, noise, cry; de hu, with noise, noisily*. The verse is satirical in tone.
l. 47, *le biau*, Shepard in *Mélanges Offerts à Alfred Jeanroy*, 1928, p. 576 suggests that *le biau* means *le beau temps*.
l. 57, *D[u]*. In the MS. there is no letter after *D*. *Du* is suggested, because it is in l. 61 under similar cir-

cumstances.
l. 59, *postulas apostole*. The Pope Clement V was crowned at Lyons in 1305, and the Pope John XXII was elected there in 1316, more than two years after the death of Clement V. The Babylonian captivity (1305-77) started with these two Popes. Clement lived at various bishoprics in France, and John definitely chose Avignon for his residence.

Du rapeler ton fait nice es et fole:	Thou art silly and crazy to call back thy action:
Donner, puis tondre, n'apartient à prodome.	To give, then to clip off, does not become an honest man.
Nous retendrons ton don; et te rigolle	We shall retain thy gift; and amuse thyself
Par de delà et tes despens asomme.	On that side, and calculate thine expenses.

IX (R.)

65 J'ai assommé: où est qui paiera?	I have calculated: Where is the one who will pay?
Parmain me faut qui fait le paiement.	On the morrow I need one who will make the payment.
Touz jourz enssi, se Dex plaist, ne sera.	It will not always be thus, if it please God.
Se chardonnaus ont ouvré malement,	If the cardinals have worked badly,
Par devers moi le tout raportera;	He[the Pope] will bring back everything to me;
70 Si sera riche plus qu'au commencement.	And he will be richer than at the beginning.
Droit à droit tourne, et le fin cuer ne ment,	Right returns to right, and the fine heart does not lie,
Et, se Dex plait, se(ce) Pape adrecera.	And, if it please God, the Pope will set that aright.

X (F.)

Fole s'i fie et fole s'i atent:	A foolish woman trusts and a foolish woman waits:
Telle es-tu, Romme, qui le cuides ravoir.	Such art thou, Rome, who thinkest to get him again.
75 De ce ta teste ne va ja debatant?	About this, is not thy head already debating?
Deça nous lesse le Pape et nostre avoir;	Here leave us the Pope and our property;
En sa terre est, si s'i va esbatant.	He is in his land, and is enjoying himself there.
[Si] du rapeler fais trop non-savoir.	So, with thy recalling thou showest too much ignorance.
Par devers toy des amis pas n'a tant	With thee he has not so many friends
80 Com devers nous. Le sien n'i veüst avoir.	As with us. His things he would not wish to have there.

---

l. 66, *Parmain*, may also mean *soon* or *shortly*, as Shepard says, *op. cit.*, p. 576.

ll. 71, 72. These two lines are written in this order in the MS. For the rhyme scheme, they should be reversed.

l. 72, *(ce) Pape adrecera*, may also mean: *He (God) will set that Pope aright*.

l. 78, [*Si*]. An additional syllable is needed for the meter.

XI (R.)

En la maniere que tu diz, doit-il estre?
Autre raison, pour moy, ne veil avoir*(requierre)*:
Le ni au Pape,— ce doit chascun conestre,—
Est où demourent et St. Pol et St. Pierre.
85 De nostre foy sunt-il le[s] greigneur mestres.
Et celui leu doit le Pape requierre;
Quer c'est le chief, c'est la partie destre,
Et c'est *l'iglise(l'Eglise)* que Dex fonda sus pierre.

In the manner that thou sayest, must it be?
Another reason, for myself, I do not wish to seek:
The home of the Pope,— every one should know this,—
Is where dwell both St. Paul and St. Peter.
Of our faith they are the greatest masters.
And this place the Pope should seek;
For it is the head, it is the right-hand part,
And it is the Church which God founded on rock.

XII (F.)

Se tu es chief, Eglise bien fondée,
90 Mal ait le chief qui ses membres ne garde!
Par devers nous est foy et loy trouvée;
Et se le Pape, qui en doit estre garde,
I est, ce n'est pas chose reprouvée.
Il est proufit que par tout il regarde;
95 Encor n'i est la cort mout demourée.
Lesse-le-nous, aten et ne te tarde.

If thou art head, well founded Church,
Woe to the head which does not guard its members!
With us faith and law are found;
And if the Pope, who should be their guard,
Is there, it is not a blamable thing.
It is beneficial that he look everywhere;
Still has the court not remained here long.
Leave him to us, wait, and be not anxious.

XIII (R.)

Ençois me tarde ceste grant demourance,
Quer en son siege et son leu proprement
Chascun evesque doit faire demourance;
100 Et cil mau fait qui le fait autrement.
Il est seus homs, le Pape: sa puissance

But this long stay makes me anxious.
For in his see and his place, properly,
Each bishop should make his stay;
And he does ill who does otherwise.
He is a single man, the Pope: his power

---

l. 82, *(requierre)*. The rhyme requires a two-syllable word in *-erre*. Because of the poet's fondness for repeating words in rhymes, *requierre* (in l. 86) is suggested.
l. 83, *ni*, literally means *nest*.

l. 89, *Eglise*, a vocative, with an ironical touch. Shepard (*op. cit.*, p. 577) suggests [*d'*]*eglise*. The verse would then read: *If thou art head of well founded Church*.
l. 101, *puissance*. See note on l. 110.

Ne peut par tout aler communement;	Cannot go everywhere at one time;
Menistres a, aux quiex de sa puissance	He has ministers, with whom he can
Departir peut à son devisement.	Share his power according to his will.

XIV (F.)

105 Departir peut, se partir peut et prendre.	He can share, (if) he can set out and can take.
Il est raison que tout ce puisse faire;	It is right that he be able to do all this;
Pour ce, di-ge qu'en ne le doit reprendre	Wherefore, I say that he should not be taken back
De quelque part que il se veille traire.	From any place whither he may wish to withdraw.
De sa puissance peut-il par tout espandre,	He can spread his power everywhere,
110 Et commander ce que li voudra plaire.	And order what he wishes, to please it.
Pour ce, conclu et à ce veu-ge tendre	Wherefore, I conclude, and to this I wish to lead,
Que touz se doivent de s'ordenance taire.	That all should be silent about his order.

XV (R.)

De s'ordenance riens ne veil ordener.	About his order I do not wish to order anything,
Mes raison moustre, et auxinc fait droiture,	But reason demonstrates, and thus does right,
115 Que là, où voudrent leur vie demener,	That there where the Saints, the Popes, wished to lead their lives,
Et d'autre part avoir leur sepouture	And furthermore have their burial,—
Les Sains, les Papes,— s'à droit veüst assener,—	If rightly he might wish to proceed,—
Là prendre doit son ni, sa reverture.	There he should take his home, his return.
S'aler n'i peut, si s'i face mener,	If he cannot go there, let him have himself taken there,
120 Quer c'est le leu de s'especial cure.	For it is the place of his special care.

XVI (F.)

D'especial evesque en s'esveschié	In his bishopric of a special bishop

---

l. 105. Shepard (*op. cit.*, p. 578) suggests that the second *peut* should read *veut*. As *partir* may mean *divide*, the verse would then read: *He can share, if he wishes to divide and take.* In the translation *if* is put in parentheses, because *se* may be a reflexive: *se partir* means *to set out, go away*.
l. 108, *ni*. See l. 83.
l. 110, *li*, refers to *puissance*, which is more or less personified in l. 109, as it is also in the preceding stanza, l. 101.

A plusieurs villes et par tout seig[n]ourie,
Et visitant s'en va de chié en chié.

En sa cité touz jourz ne remaint mie;
125 Aussi seroit et mau fait et pechié,

Se le Pape iere touz jourz en Rommenie.
Il doit aller et venir derechié,
Si peut par tout où il a seignourie.

XVII

Sa seignourie par tout s'estent sanz doute,
130 Mes la puissance d'un evesque est petite;
Si ne peut pas la cretienté toute

Un visiter; ne raison ne le dite.
Commander peut, et droit est qu'en l'escoute.
Par ses menistres va par tout et habite;
135 Et ce souffire doit assez,— nul n'en doute.
Et vieingne à Romme, quer à tort la despite.

XVIII

Ençois à cause et loial et certainne

Te despit, Romme, le Pape, et te descline;
Quar tu as pris et la char et la lainne
140 De tout le monde par usure et rapine,
Par simonie, dont tu as esté plaine,

Par tricherie et mauvaise couvine.
Si t'en bat Dex de semaine en semaine,
Ne devers toi la court ne s'achemine.

He has several cities and everywhere seigniory,
And he goes visiting from one end to the other [of his see].

In his stronghold he does not always stay;
So, it would be both ill-done and wrong,

If the Pope were always in the territory of Rome.
He should go and come again,
And he may go everywhere where he has seigniory.

(R.)

His seigniory extends everywhere, doubtless,
But the power of a bishop is slight;
And one person cannot visit all Christianity;

Nor does reason so dictate.
He may command, and it is right for one to listen to him.
Through his ministers he goes and dwells everywhere;
And this should be quite sufficient,— no one doubts it.
And let him come to Rome, for wrongly he scorns her.

(F.)

Rather, for a reason both loyal and certain,

The Pope scorns thee, Rome, and avoids thee;
For thou hast taken both the flesh (food) and the wool (clothing)
Of everybody by usury and rapine,
By simony, of which thou hast been full,

By trickery and evil project.
So, God beats thee for that from week to week,
Nor does the court proceed towards thee.

---

l. 122, *a. He*, the subject of *a*, means the "especial evesque."

l. 123, *de chié en chié*, is a form of *de chief en chief*.

XIX (R.)

145 Qui reprens-tu d'usure et d'ava-
rice?
Regarde-toy: Sus toy trop a à dire.

Conchiée es d'om; chascun de ce vice
Est plus que moy; *de venue(devenue) enespire(en es pire)*.
Par tout le monde voi regner malefice;
150 Des mauvais vient,— ce ne peut [-en] desdire,—
Quer par tout [le] seme li fol et nice;
Si s'en peut pou li un de l'autre rire.

Whom art thou reproving for usury and avarice?
Look at thyself: About thee there is too much to say.

Thou art sullied by man; every one by this vice
Is characterized more than I; thou art become worse therefrom.
Through all the world I see crime reign;
From the evil ones it comes,— this cannot be refuted,—
For everywhere the fool and simpleton sow it;
So, one can laugh very little at another.

XX (F.)

Ençois m'en ri et m'en moque, sanz faille,
De toi, quar j'ai le noiau, tu l'escorce;
155 Par devers moy le grain, tu as la paille.
A bonne cause de toy me ri; pour ce,
Ne requier plus que la court à toy aille;
D'aler à toy le Pape n'i fait force.

Il a deça bons vins, bonne vitaille,
160 Gent qui d'amer et lui servir s'efforce.

Rather do I laugh and make fun of thee, without fail,
For I have the kernel, thou the shell;
With me is the grain, thou hast the straw.
With good reason I laugh at thee; wherefore,
Seek not longer to have the court go to thee;
The Pope does not trouble himself about going to thee.

He has here good wines, good food,
People who strive to love and serve him.

XXI (R.)

De ta vitaille, ne de ta garnison,

Force n'i fais. N'ai-ge vins et viandes?
Pour tes grans robes cuides que te prison?

I am not troubled about thy food, nor about thy provisions.
Have I not wines and viands?
For thy great booty thinkest thou that we esteem thee?

---

l. 145, *avarice*, is also berated in *Les Avisemens*, ll. 948, 979, 1000.
l. 148, *de venue*, means *immediately*. If *enespire* were a p.p. (which the rhyme does not permit) meaning *instilled*, and the preceding words were changed to *moy devenu*, the reading would be:

Has more than I become instilled.
ll. 150, 151, *(en) . . . (le)*. An additional syllable is needed for the meter in each verse.
l. 155, *grain . . . paille*. Cf. *Les Avisemens*, l. 610.

Grec et Garnache avon que tu demandes.	We have Greek wine and Grenache for which thou asketh.
165 Mes trop feroit le Pape mesprison,	But the Pope would make too great a mistake,
S'il est chiez toy pour prendre tes offrandes.	If he is in thy country to take thy offerings.
Et si croion et ainsi le dison	And so we believe and thus we say so,
Qu'assez petit de sa presence amendes.	That thou givest rather little compensation for his presence.

XXII (F.)

Et que te chaut de mon amendement?	And what matters my compensation to thee?
170 Par devers nous le lesse demourer.	With us let him stay.
Tes chardonnaus de leur consentement	Thy cardinals with their consent
Venu deça sont Saint Pierre aourer;	Have come here to adore Saint Peter;
Et d'Anthioche vint Saint Pierre ensement	And from Antioch came Saint Peter likewise
De sa presence son païs honorer.	To honor his country with his presence.
175 Dont, se le Pape par son ordenement	Therefore, if the Pope by his arrangement
Est par deça, de ce ne dois plourer.	Is here, about that thou shouldst not lament.

XXIII (R.)

S'à Romme vint Saint Pierre d'Anthioche,	If Saint Peter came to Rome from Antioch,
Ceste ordenance de par Dieu en fu faite:	This arrangement was made by God:
C'est la maison qui fondée est sus roche,	It is the house which is founded upon rock,
180 Qui vent ne doute, pluye, assaut, ne retraite.	Which fears not wind, rain, assault, nor retreats (falls).
Se chardonnaus m'ont fait honte et reprouche,	If cardinals have caused me shame and reproach,
L'ordenance de Dieu, qui est parfaite,	The arrangement of God, which is perfect,
Doit demourer estable et ferme en coche,	Should remain stable and firm as a notch,
Ne par nul home ne doit estre deffaite.	Nor by any man should it be undone.

XXIV (F.)

185 Or m'as-tu point sanz pointure de mouche;	Now thou hast stung me without the sting of a fly;

1. 164, *Grec et Garnache*. Shepard, *op. cit.*, p. 580, cites several cases where these two names of wines are coupled.

Garnache also means *smock-frock*.
ll. 179-80. This Biblical figure is also found in *Les Alliés*, ll. 63-72.

Ce que tu diz est de congruïté,
Et nequedant en jugement me couche,
Que ce n'est pas cas de necessité.
Or faisons pais, chascun cloe sa bouche;
190 Nus sommes seurs, soions en amité;
Et nostre pere,—c'est Dex, à cui il touche,—
Ce en face où plus ara d'utilité.

XXV

Quant tu *feüst(feüs)* au pont, auxi [i] fu-ge;
C'est un proverbe que souvent l'en recorde;
195 Nous sommes seurs, or lessons ce deluge,
Quer nous devons pais amer et concorde.
De noz contemps Dieu le souverain Juge
En ordenoit, car du tout m'i acorde;
Il me plaist bien que celui nous en juge:
200 Je ne veil plus avoir à toy descorde.

What thou sayest is consistent,
And nevertheless I incline in judgment,
For it is not a case of necessity.
Now let us make peace, let each close her mouth;
We are sisters, let us be friends;
And may our Father,— that is God, Whom it concerns,—
Dispose of him where he will have most usefulness.

(R.)

When thou wast at the bridge, also I was there;
That is a proverb which is often recalled.
We are sisters, now let us leave this flood [of words],
For we should love peace and concord.
May God, the sovereign Judge, settle our quarrels,
For I am entirely in accord;
I am well pleased that He should judge us:
I wish to have no more discord with thee.

---

l. 193, [i]. This additional syllable, needed for the meter, is suggested by Shepard, *op cit.*, p. 581, who thinks that the meaning of the proverb is:

"Nous sommes égaux, du même âge."
l. 198, *ordenoit*, pres. subj.; see l. 378 of *Un Songe.*

LIST OF PROPER NAMES OF PERSONS AND OF PLACES

Abbreviations

AL. *Les Alliés*
AV. *Les Avisemens*
C. *De la Comete*
D. *Desputoison*
P. *Du Roy Phelippe*
S. *Un Songe*

Ajax, AV. 1183. Greek hero at the siege of Troy.
Alexandre,-s, AV. 748, 752, 753. Alexander the Great (356-323 B.C.), King of Macedonia.
Anglois, AV. 491. The English.
Anthioche, D. 173, 177. Antioch, city of Syria.
Aristote, AV. 751; C. 132. Aristotle, Greek philosopher (384-322 B.C.).
Ath -aines, -eines, -einnes, AV. 623, 626, 628. Athens, capital of Greece.

Brie, AV. 527, Region of France between the Seine and Marne Rivers.

Challemaine, AV. 343, 668, 672. Charlemagne, King of the Franks, and Emperor of the Occident (800-814).
Charlle, AV. 370. See Challemaine.
Climence, C. 309, 319. Clémence de Hongrie, second wife of Louis X of France.
Conradin, AV. 453. Duke of Swabia, decapitated in 1268 in Naples.
Constentin, AV. 386. Constantine, first Christian Emperor of Rome (272-337).
Courtai, AV. 1133. Courtrai, city of Flanders where Philip IV of France was defeated in 1302 by the Flemings.
Crestiens, S. 171; C. 54. The Christians.

Dagoubert, AV. 410. Dagobert, King of the Franks (623-632).
David, AV. 820. King of Israel, writer of the *Psalms*.
Denis, see Saint Denis.

Espeingne, C. 174. Spain.
Eve, S. 157. Wife of Adam.

Federi, AV. 454. Probably Frederick II, Emperor of the Holy Roman Empire, who was excommunicated by the pope and died in 1250.
Flamenz, C. 141, 146. The Flemings.
Flandres, AV. 491. Flanders.
France, AV. 413, 527, 575, 670, 674, 878, 954, 1134, 1224; S. 375; AL. 244; C. 8, 20, 98, 103, 133, 154, 171, 213, 218, 238, 239, 252, 323.

Galilee, AL. 216. Ancient Roman province of N. Palestine.
Ganelon, AL. 82. Traitor in the *Chanson de Roland*.
Gascoigne, C. 173. Gascony, region of S. W. France.
Geffroy de Paris, AV. 1359. Author of the six poems.
Godefroy de Buillon, AV. 476. Godfrey of Bouillon, leader of the First Crusade (1096-1100).
Gregois, AV. 1180. The Greeks.
Gui d'Aucerre, AV. 1037. Guy, Bishop of Auxerre (933-961).

Jeroboem, AV. 919. Jeroboam, a Jewish leader who led the revolt of the ten tribes against Rehoboam (I Kings, XI, XII).
Jerusalem, AV. 901.
Jherusalem, S. 178. Jerusalem.
Jhesu Crist, S. 272. Jesus Christ.
Joan, S. 282. Pope John XXII (1316-1334).
Johan, P. 3. John I, posthumous son of Louis X, and French king for the several days of his life in November, 1316.
Juif, AV. 506. See Juys.
Julien Cesar, AV. 742. Julius Caesar, Roman leader (100-44 B.C.).
Justinien, AV. 759, 1200. Justinian, Roman Emperor of the East (483-565).
Juys, AV. 265, 517; S. 171. The Jews.

Lombars, S. 175. The Lombards, famous as money lenders and usurers, from N. Italy.
Louvre, S. 345. Royal palace in Paris.
Loÿs (IX) (Saint), AV. 426, 433, 1158. Louis IX, King of France (1226-1270).
Loÿs (X), AV. 458, 976; P. 3, 5; C. 139, 145. Louis X, King of France (1314-1316).

Machabées, AV. 537. The Maccabees, a Jewish family of patriots of the 2nd century B.C.
Mahom, AV. 264. Mohammed, Arabian religious leader (570-632). The name is also used to refer to any non-Christian religious leader.
Mainfroi, AV. 453. Manfred, King of Naples, killed in battle in 1266.
Morise, see Saint Morise.
Moÿses, AV. 508. Moses, Jewish leader (1571-1451 B.C.).

Naimes, AV. 1033. Naimon, counsellor of Charlemagne in the *Chanson de Roland*.

Paris, AV. 1163, 1273.
Pharaon, AV. 265. Pharaoh, King of ancient Egypt.
Phelippe (IV), P. 3. Philip IV, King of France (1285-1314), father of Louis X, Philip V, and Charles IV.
Phelippe (V); P. 5, 71, 113; S. 349. Philip V, King of France (1316-22), second son of Philip IV, succeeded his nephew John I in November, 1316.
Pierre, see Saint Pierre.
Pilatus Pocius, AV. 425. Pontius Pilate, Roman official in Judea A.D. 26.
Poitiers, S. 299. City of W. France.
Pol, see Saint Pol.

Robo -am, -em, AV. 901, 918. Rehoboam, son of Solomon, from whom the ten tribes revolted (II Chron. IX, 31).
Rommains, AV. 639. The Romans.
Romme, AV. 632, 635, 646, 652, 662, 667, 671, 673; D. 1, 9, 37, 58, 74, 136, 138, 177. Rome.
Rommenie D. 126. Romagna, territory around Rome.

Saint Denis, AV. 418. Patron saint of France.
Saint Denise, C. 195. Saint Denis, city north of Paris, burial place of French kings.
Saint Morise, AV. 418. Saint Maurice, martyred saint of the 3rd century.
Saint Pierre, D. 84, 172, 173, 177. Saint Peter, one of the twelve apostles.
Saint Pol, D. 84. Saint Paul, Saul of Tarsus.
Salemon, -t, AV. 49, 813, 822, 902. Solomon, son of David, King of Israel (1033-975 B.C.).

Temple, S. 345. Seat of the Templars in Paris.
Templiers, S. 171. The Knights Templar, military order founded in the 12th century and suppressed by the Council of Vienne in 1312 at the instigation of Philip IV of France.
Theodosius, AV. 424. Roman Emperor of the East (379-395).
Troie, AV. 628, 1175, 1179. Troy, ancient city of Asia Minor.
Turpin, AV. 1035. Charlemagne's archbishop in the *Chanson de Roland*.

Ulixes, AV. 1186, 1189. Ulysses, Greek hero in the Trojan war.

Ysaïe, AL. 220. Isaiah, Hebrew prophet, lived about 720 B.C.

www.ingramcontent.com/pod-product-compliance
Lightning Source LLC
Chambersburg PA
CBHW030234240426
43663CB00036B/441